Christmas Treasury for Children

First published in 1995 by
Marino Books
An imprint of Mercier Press
16 Hume Street Dublin 2

Trade enquiries to Mercier Press
PO Box 5, 5 French Church Street,
Cork

© Rose Doyle 1995 introduction and all pieces not otherwise attributed. The acknowledgements page is an extension of this copyright notice

ISBN 1 86023 035 0

10 9 8 7 6 5 4 3 2 1

A CIP record for this title is available from the British Library

Cover collage and design
by Brian Finnegan
Set by Richard Parfrey
Printed in Ireland by ColourBooks,
Baldoyle Industrial Estate, Dublin 13

This book is sold subject to the condition that it shall not, by way of trade or otherwise, be lent, resold, hired out or otherwise circulated without the publisher's prior consent in any form of binding or cover other than that in which it is published and without a similar condition including this condition being imposed on the subsequent purchaser.

No part of this publication may be reproduced or transmitted in any form or by any means, electronic or mechanical, including photocopying, recording or any information or retrieval system, without the prior permission of the publisher in writing.

Christmas Treasury for Children

Edited by Rose Doyle

Contents

Introduction		7
'For Unto Us a Child Is Born'	Isaiah	11
The Fat Boy's Christmas	Maeve Binchy	12
The Little Match-Girl	Hans Christian Andersen	17
The Night Before Christmas	Clement Clarke Moore	21
Santa Claus		24
His First Christmas Dinner	James Joyce	26
Before the Paling of the Stars	Christina Rossetti	32
The Christmas Star		34
The Twelve Days of Christmas	Anon	35
December Diary	George and Weedon Grossmith	40
Songs in Season	Anon	43
Snow Pancakes		45
The Season of Light	Éamon Kelly	46
Christmas at Sea	Robert Louis Stevenson	51
Holly and Ivy and All That Greenery		55
Christmas with the Savages	Mary Clive	56
Oíche Nollag	Máire Mhac an tSaoi	60
The Christmas Tree		61
Last Bus for Christmas	Patricia Lynch	62
Once in Royal David's City	Cecil Frances Alexander	71
The Twelve Days of Christmas, A Correspondence	John Julius Norwich	74
The Christmas Stocking		78
Scrooge's Christmas Day	Charles Dickens	79
Christmas Presents		88

from A Christmas Childhood	Patrick Kavanagh	89
A Merry Christmas	Thomás Ó Crohan	91
A Christmas Carol	G. K. Chesterton	96
Christmas Delicacies – US Style		97
The Friar's Christmas Night	Sean Henry	98
I Sing Of A Maiden	Anon	100
The Crib		101
The Christmas of Samuel Pepys		102
The Road to Heaven	George R. Sims	103
Christmas Cards		110
The Fir Tree	Tove Jansson	111
The Yuletide Log		121
An Austrian Christmas	Maria Von Trapp	122
While Shepherds Watched Their Flocks By Night	Nahum Tate	128
Christmas Seals		130
Cuireadh do Mhuire	Máirtín Ó Direáin	131
Christmas in Europe		132
A Comfortable Christmas	Charles Dickens	133
Santa on the Internet	Gordon Snell	136
Christmas Carols		139
Angel Children	Louisa May Alcott	140
The Christmas-Tree	Julia Goddard	147
Glory to God in the Highest	The Gospel of St Luke	150
Adeste, Fideles	Anon	152
Biographical Index		153
Acknowledgements		160

Introduction

> At Christmas play and make good cheer,
> For Christmas comes but once a year.

It's more than four hundred years since Thomas Tusser passed on this piece of advice. It was a bit unnecessary – most people have never needed to be told that Christmas is a time to celebrate and enjoy, to give as well as to take and generally get in touch with the nicer side of life and ourselves.

Most people, but not everyone. There are the Scrooges who, like wet weather, are always with us and who moan that once a year is too often. This book is not for them. It's for the rest of us, the vast majority who, in spite of the killjoys, put a lot of energy into play and cheer for this wintertime festival. In its pages you will find stories, poems, lore and legends, some happy and some sad, all of them to do with Christmas. Maeve Binchy has written a special story too. It's full of Maeve's warmth and wit and you're sure to love it.

When making the selection I tried for as broad a range of seasonal writings as possible. A lot are old, in the sense that they've been around for a long time. But then too so has Christmas – since the fourth century at the latest, when it became a Christian substitute for the pagan festival of 25 December, which was a celebration of the birth of the unconquered sun. You didn't know that? There's a lot more to be discovered when you read on.

All through this Treasury you'll find word of the reason

we celebrate Christmas today. An anonymous carol put it most simply of all:

> Remember Christ Our Saviour,
> Who was born on Christmas Day.

Amongst the poems are Robert Louis Stevenson's 'Christmas at Sea', sad and fierce, a-rage with the fury of a sea-storm and melancholy with images of a cottage and firelight on 'blessed Christmas Day.' Patrick Kavanagh's 'A Christmas Childhood' gives us long-ago sounds of the countryside. Sights too, as in 'In silver the wonder of a Christmas townland/The winking glitter of a frosty dawn.'

There is a piece from James Joyce's *A Portrait of the Artist as a Young Man*, included for the wonderful images it gives of a Dublin Christmas Day a hundred years ago. Scrooge's Christmas Day is here, of course, because Dickens was a master of atmosphere and evoked, as here, joy and misery so well. There are stories too from Éamon Kelly and Patricia Lynch, writers who bring old country ways at this time of year to exciting life.

Some poems have a history. 'The Night before Christmas' is one. It was written in 1823 by Clement C. Moore, an American poet and professor of theology. In it he gave Santa Claus reindeer, a sleigh and white beard – and the world a new image of a character who, until then, had been seen as a kindly Dutchman in breeches.

The Danish writer Hans Christian Andersen is represented by a sad story. He wrote 'The Little Match-Girl' to prove that his stories were universal and not simply intended for children. I hadn't read it since I was a small child myself and now, reading it again, I see that Andersen was right. His story, bitter as well as sad and telling about poverty and the outcast in society, is for everyone. I've also included a story by Tove Jansson about the Moomintrolls, creatures of the Finnish forests. It seemed only right that there should be something from the Scandinavian countries we associate so much with the season.

There are two versions of 'The Twelve Days of Christmas'. One is traditional and the other, by John Julius Norwich, is in the form of an hilarious correspondence – with a disastrous ending you can see coming from day three.

There is more – enough, I hope, to keep everyone happy. So, as Sir Walter Scott admonished:

> Heap on more wood! the wind is chill;
> But let it whistle as it will.
> We'll keep our Christmas merry still.

And have a great Christmas read.

'or Unto Us a Child Is Born'

The passage which fortells the Nativity of Christ comes from Isaiah 9: 6-7. It is full of glorious promise.

For unto us a child is born, unto us a son is given: and the government shall be upon his shoulder: and his name shall be called Wonderful, Counsellor, The mighty God, The everlasting Father, The Prince of Peace. Of the increase of his government and peace there shall be no end, upon the throne of David, and upon his kingdom, to order it, and to establish it with judgement and with justice from henceforth even for ever. The zeal of the Lord of hosts will perform this.

The Fat Boy's Christmas

MAEVE BINCHY

Freddie was a fat boy. And to make matters worse, his father and mother had called him Frederick Andrew when he was a baby, forgetting that their name was Tobin and so his initials would always be F. A. T.

In Freddie's school they had to have initials on things, like their sports bags and the paper covers on their textbooks and people always laughed when they saw big Freddie carrying a bag marked F. A. T.

'As if we didn't know,' said Kevin Daly, who was terrific at games and ate mountains of chips and crisps, and could run and leap like the wind.

'You don't need to tell us, Freddie, you don't have to advertise it,' said Orla, who was the most gorgeous girl in the school and who could run and jump as well as Kevin – and she was never seen without an ice cream cone in her hand.

Freddie thought it was all very unfair. He didn't eat all those things he would have loved so much because they were bad for his heart. He got no praise for passing when the fizzy orange was offered, or for saying no to the chocolate biscuits he would have loved. 'I'll bet Freddie eats tons and tons of those when he's on his own,' they said.

Every year for a while now Freddie had written to Santa Claus and asked for something that would make him thin. He didn't know what it would be – a pill, a powder, a magic wand, a spell. Whatever it took. But somehow Santa Claus never brought it. Either it didn't exist, or he didn't think it was really serious. Everything else that Santa Claus brought to Freddie and his brother and sister was terrific. He got a Walkman and he got a nice sturdy bicycle so Santa Claus must have known he was heavy.

When Freddie was nine and a half, he decided that Santa Claus hadn't really understood how desperate the situation was becoming. School was a misery these days: there had been no part for him in the school play; obviously he hadn't been in the gymnastics display; he had been invited to one Christmas party but then it had been spoiled because somebody said they'd all have to get there early in case Freddie ate all the food.

So he began a long letter to Santa Claus, explaining that it didn't matter about the other gifts but he would very much like to be thin. He told Santa Claus about how great it would be to run and jump over things and to be picked for teams and to be able to wear other people's shirts if he had lost his own.

He was just finishing the letter when his Uncle Spekky arrived. Uncle Spekky came for Christmas whenever he was in Ireland but that wasn't often because he was a famous pop star now, he had his own band, Spekky's Sound, and he sang with them, and he could be in Las Vegas or Australia. He was of course seriously old, like in his twenties or something, but not as old as Freddie's parents. Nobody at school knew that Freddie had anything to do with Spekky's Sound. For one thing they might laugh at him and say he had eaten all their dinners and that's why the members of Spekky's Sound were all so thin, and for another, he could never prove it because Uncle Spekky didn't say when he was coming to visit as he was a bit unreliable.

Uncle Spekky was small and wore huge red-framed glasses. 'What are you asking for? All my new records I hope?' he said.

'Not exactly,' Freddie told him.

You could talk to Uncle Spekky quite easily – he wasn't grown up or young – so Freddie told him about the letter and the many misunderstandings over the years. He felt sure his uncle would understand.

'I don't think they can give you that kind of thing at Christmas. I used to ask for better eyes so that I could see properly without squinting but Santa Claus never gave them. I imagine they can't have it in stock.'

'Ah, but that was different!' Freddie said.

'No it wasn't. There was a fellow in my school, a real tough guy called Monty Johnson who called me Spekky Four Eyes because I wore such thick glasses. I used to want to tell him that if I could see properly I wouldn't wear them but I never dared. So in the end I pretended I liked wearing them, and that's what gives me my name now.'

Freddie was amazed. He had always thought his uncle had been named Spekky at his christening.

'So what did you ask for instead?' Freddie asked.

'I asked for a guitar,' said Spekky, one of the world's

most famous guitar players.

'What do you think I should ask for?' Freddie wondered.

'A cheap computer, the cheapest one they have, so that you can get started.'

'Started on what, Uncle Spekky?'

'I need someone to run my junior fan club. Could you do it?'

'Yes but would they . . . I mean they mightn't . . . you don't know . . . '

Freddie couldn't find the words to tell his uncle that he was the wrong person to be in charge of something that Kevin and Orla would be so impressed by. But suddenly he knew there was something he must ask.

'Whatever happened to Monty, you know the one who called you names?'

'He's my roadie. He packs the vans; he unpacks them; he works for me, Freddie. He calls himself M. T. J. He has it on his T-shirts.'

There was a silence. It seemed too impressive, too far from Freddie.

'Monty Timothy Johnson . . . that's his name now. He added the Timothy bit,' said Uncle Spekky.

'My initials aren't much good.' Freddie was apologetic. 'They didn't know how things were going to be. My initials are F. A. T.'

Now everything had been told.

'You could add another name, like Monty did. You could add Sean. Call yourself F. A. S. T. – Fast Freddie. I'd be proud to have someone called Fast Freddie on my team.'

That year Freddie asked for a cheap computer from Santa Claus for Christmas. He could hardly wait for the new term to begin.

The Little Match-Girl

HANS CHRISTIAN ANDERSEN

It was so dreadfully cold! It was snowing, and the evening was beginning to darken. It was the last evening of the year, too – New Year's Eve. Through the cold and the dark, a poor little girl with bare head and naked feet was wandering along the road. She had, indeed, had a pair of slippers on when she left home; but what was the good of that! They were very big slippers – her mother had worn them last, they were so big – and the little child had lost them hurrying across the road as two carts rattled dangerously past. One slipper could not be found, and a boy ran off with the other – he said he could use it as a cradle when he had children of his own.

So the little girl wandered along with her naked little feet red and blue with cold. She was carrying a great pile of matches in an old apron and she held one bundle in her hand as she walked. No one had bought a thing from her the whole day; no one had given her a halfpenny; hungry and frozen, she went her way, looking so woebegone, poor little thing! The snow-flakes fell upon her long fair hair that curled so prettily about the nape of her neck, but she certainly wasn't thinking of how nice she looked. Lights were shining from all the windows, and there was a lovely smell of roast goose all down the street, for it was indeed New Year's Eve – yes, and that's what she was thinking about.

Over in a corner between two houses, where one jutted a little farther out into the street than the other, she sat down and huddled together; she had drawn her little legs up under her, but she felt more frozen than ever, and she dared not go home, for she had sold no matches and hadn't got a single penny, and her father would beat her. Besides, it was cold at home, too: there was only the roof over them, and the wind whistled in, although the biggest cracks had been stopped up with straw and rags. Her little hands were almost dead with cold. Ah, a little match might do some good! If she only dared pull one out of the bundle, strike it on the wall, and warm her fingers! She drew one out – Whoosh! – How it spluttered! How it burnt! It gave a warm bright flame, just like a little candle, when she held her hand round it. It was wonderful light: the little girl thought she was sitting in front of a great iron stove with polished brass knobs and fittings; the fire was burning so cheerfully and its warmth was so comforting – oh, what was that! The little girl had just stretched her feet out to warm them, too, when – the fire went out! The stove disappeared – and she was sitting there with the little stump of a burnt-out match in her hand.

Another match was struck, it burnt and flared, and where the light fell upon it, the wall became transparent like gauze; she could see right into the room where the table stood covered with a shining white cloth and set with fine china, and there was a roast goose, stuffed with prunes and apples, steaming deliciously – but what was more gorgeous still, the goose jumped off the dish, waddled across the floor with knife and fork in its back, and went straight over to the poor girl. Then the match went out, and there was nothing to see but the thick cold wall.

She struck yet another. And then she was sitting beneath the loveliest Christmas tree; it was even bigger and more beautifully decorated than the one she had seen this last Christmas through the glass doors of the wealthy grocer's shop. Thousands of candles were burning on its green branches, and gaily coloured pictures, like those that had decorated the shop-windows, were looking down at her. The little girl stretched out both her hands – and then the match went out; the multitude of Christmas-candles rose higher and higher, and now she saw they were the bright stars – one of them fell and made a long streak of fire across the sky.

'Someone's now dying!' said the little girl, for her old granny, who was the only one that had been kind to her, but who was now dead, had said that when a star falls a soul goes up to God.

Once more she struck a match on the wall. It lit up the darkness round about her, and in its radiance stood old granny, so bright and shining, so wonderfully kind.

'Granny!' cried the little girl. 'Oh, take me with you! I know you'll go away when the match goes out – you'll go away just like the warm stove and the lovely roast goose and the wonderful big Christmas tree!' – And she hastily struck all the rest of the matches in the bundle, for she wanted to keep her granny there, and the matches shone with such brilliance that it was brighter than daylight. Granny had never before been so tall and beautiful; she lifted the little girl up on her arm, and they flew away in splendour and joy, high high up towards heaven. And there was no more cold and no more hunger and no more fear – they were with God.

But in the corner of the house, in the cold of the early morning, the little girl sat, with red cheeks and a smile upon her lips – dead, frozen to death on the last evening of the old year. The morning of the New Year rose over the little dead body sitting there with her matches, one bundle nearly all burnt out. She wanted to keep herself warm, they said; but no one knew what beautiful things she had seen, nor in what radiance she had gone with her old granny into the joy of the New Year.

The Night Before Christmas

CLEMENT CLARKE MOORE

'Twas the night before Christmas, when all through the house
Not a creature was stirring, not even a mouse;
The stockings were hung by the chimney with care,
In hopes that St Nicholas soon would be there;
The children were nestled all snug in their beds,
While visions of sugar-plums danced in their heads;
And mamma in her 'kerchief, and I in my cap,
Had just settled our brains for a long winter's nap –
When out on the lawn there arose such a clatter,
I sprang from my bed to see what was the matter.
Away to the window I flew like a flash,
Tore open the shutters, and threw up the sash.
The moon, on the breast of the new-fallen snow,
Gave the lustre of midday to objects below;
When, what to my wondering eyes should appear,
But a miniature sleigh and eight tiny reindeer,
With a little old driver, so lively and quick,
I knew in a moment it must be St Nick.
More rapid than eagles his coursers they came,
And he whistled, and shouted, and called them by name:

'Now, *Dasher*! now, *Dancer*! now, *Prancer* and *Vixen*!
On, *Comet*! on, *Cupid*! on, *Donder* and *Blitzen*!
To the top of the porch! to the top of the wall!
Now dash away! dash away! dash away all!'
As dry leaves that before the wild hurricane fly,
When they meet with an obstacle, mount to the sky;
So up to the house-top the coursers they flew
With the sleigh full of toys, and St Nicholas too.
And then, in a twinkling, I heard on the roof
The prancing and pawing of each little hoof –
As I drew in my head, and was turning around,
Down the chimney St Nicholas came with a bound.
He was dressed all in fur, from his head to his foot,
And his clothes were all tarnished with ashes and soot;
A bundle of toys he had flung on his back,
And he looked like a pedlar just opening his pack.
His eyes – how they twinkled; his dimples, how merry!
His cheeks were like roses, his nose like a cherry!
His droll little mouth was drawn up like a bow,
And the beard of his chin was as white as the snow;
The stump of a pipe he held tight in his teeth,
And the smoke it encircled his head like a wreath;
He had a broad face and a little round belly
That shook, when he laughed, like a bowl full of jelly.
He was chubby and plump, a right jolly old elf,
And I laughed when I saw him, in spite of myself;
A wink of his eye and a twist of his head
Soon gave me to know I had nothing to dread;
He spoke not a word, but went straight to his work,
And he filled all the stockings; then turned with a jerk,

And laying his finger aside of his nose,
And giving a nod, up the chimney he rose;
He sprang to his sleigh, to his team gave a whistle,
And away they all flew like the down of a thistle.
But I heard him exclaim, 'ere he drove out of sight,
'*Happy Christmas to all, and to all a good night!*'

anta Claus

The origins of Santa Claus are steeped in legend and myth. His name and his generous way with children at Christmas can be traced to an early Christian saint called Nicholas.

Nicholas, who lived in Asia Minor some time between 280 AD and 350 AD, was bishop of Myra and famous for his love and kindness to children and for going about in disguise, giving presents to the poor. He became a legend in his lifetime.

He had been dead seven hundred years before his fame really began to spread, though. In the eleventh century, his remains were removed and enshrined in a church in Bari, in southern Italy. This became a place of pilgrimage and Crusaders who visited brought stories about St Nicholas back to their homelands. In Germany he became know as Sankt Nikolaus or Kriss Kringle and in Holland they called him Saint Nikolaas or Sinterklaas. Dutch colonists carried the legend to America in the seventeenth century and it was there that English settlers came up with the name Santa Claus.

The Dutch Sinterklaas was a small, fat man in knee-breeches and broad-brimmed hat. It was Clement C. Moore, in his 1823 poem 'The Night Before Christmas' (which you have just read), who added the first details of the Santa Claus we know and love, including the reindeer and sleigh. Forty years later, in 1863, cartoonist Thomas Nast, in a picture for *Harper's Weekly*, gave the saint the red, fur-trimmed suit which has been his garb ever since.

 is First Christmas Dinner

FROM
A PORTRAIT OF THE ARTIST
AS A YOUNG MAN

JAMES JOYCE

A great fire, banked high and red, flamed in the grate and under the ivytwined branches of the chandelier the Christmas table was spread. They had come home a little late and still dinner was not ready: but it would be ready in a jiffy his mother had said. They were waiting for the door to open and for the servants to come in, holding the big dishes covered with their heavy metal covers.

All were waiting: uncle Charles, who sat far away in the shadow of the window, Dante and Mr Casey, who sat in the easy-chairs at either side of the hearth, Stephen, seated on a chair between them, his feet resting on the toasted boss. Mr Dedalus looked at himself in the pierglass above the mantelpiece, waxed out his moustache ends and then, parting his coat-tails, stood with his back to the glowing fire: and still from time to time he withdrew a hand from his coat-tail to wax out one of his moustache ends. Mr Casey leaned his head to one side and, smiling, tapped the gland of his neck with his fingers. And Stephen smiled too for he knew now that it was not true that Mr Casey had a purse of silver in his throat. He smiled to think how the silvery noise which Mr Casey used to make had deceived him. And when he had tried to open Mr Casey's hand to see if the purse of silver was hidden there he had seen that the fingers could not be straightened out: and Mr Casey had told him that he had got those three cramped fingers making a birthday present for Queen Victoria. Mr Casey tapped the gland of his neck and smiled at Stephen with sleepy eyes: and Mr Dedalus said to him:

– Yes. Well now, that's all right. O, we had a good walk, hadn't we, John? Yes . . . I wonder if there's any likelihood of dinner this evening. Yes . . . O, well now, we got a good breath of ozone round the Head today. Ay, bedad.

He turned to Dante and said:

– You didn't stir out at all, Mrs Riordan?

Dante frowned and said shortly:

– No.

Mr Dedalus dropped his coat-tails and went over to the sideboard. He brought forth a great stone jar of whisky from the locker and filled the decanter slowly, bending now and then to see how much he had poured in. Then replacing the jar in the locker he poured a little of the whiskey into two glasses, added a little water and came back with them to the fireplace.

– A thimbleful, John, he said, just to whet your appetite.

Mr Casey took the glass, drank, and placed it near him on the mantelpiece. Then he said:

– Well, I can't help thinking of our friend Christopher

manufacturing . . .

He broke into a fit of laughter and coughing and added:

– . . . manufacturing that champagne for those fellows.

Mr Dedalus laughed loudly.

– Is it Christy? he said. There's more cunning in one of those warts on his bald head than in a pack of jack foxes.

He inclined his head, closed his eyes, and, licking his lips profusely, began to speak with the voice of the hotel keeper.

– And he has such a soft mouth when he's speaking to you, don't you know. He's very moist and watery about the dewlaps, God bless him.

Mr Casey was still struggling through his fit of coughing and laughter. Stephen, seeing and hearing the hotel keeper through his father's face and voice, laughed.

Mr Dedalus put up his eyeglass and, staring down at him, said quietly and kindly:

– What are you laughing at, you little puppy, you?

The servants entered and placed the dishes on the table. Mrs Dedalus followed and the places were arranged.

– Sit over, she said.

Mr Dedalus went to the end of the table and said:

– Now, Mrs Riordan, sit over. John, sit you down, my hearty.

He looked round to where uncle Charles sat and said:

– Now then, sir, there's a bird here waiting for you.

When all had taken their seats he laid his hand on the cover and then said quickly, withdrawing it:

– Now, Stephen.

Stephen stood up in his place to say the grace before meals:

Bless us, O Lord, and these Thy gifts which through Thy bounty we are about to receive through Christ our Lord. Amen.

All blessed themselves and Mr Dedalus with a sigh of pleasure lifted from the dish the heavy cover pearled around the edge with glistening drops.

Stephen looked at the plump turkey which had lain, trussed and skewered, on the kitchen table. He knew that his father had paid a guinea for it in Dunn's of D'Olier Street and that the man had prodded it often at the breastbone to show how good it was: and he remembered the man's voice when he had said:

– Take that one, sir. That's real Ally Daly.

Why did Mr Barret in Clongowes call his pandybat a turkey? But Clongowes was far away: and the warm heavy smell of turkey and ham and celery rose from the plates and dishes and the great fire was banked high and red in the grate and the green ivy and red holly made you feel so happy and when dinner was ended the big plum pudding would be carried in, studded with peeled almonds and sprigs of holly, with bluish fire running around it and a little green flag flying from the top.

It was his first Christmas dinner and he thought of his little brothers and sisters who were waiting in the nursery, as he had often waited, till the pudding came. The deep low collar and the Eton jacket made him feel queer and oldish: and that morning when his mother had brought him down to the parlour, dressed for mass, his father had cried. That was because he was thinking of his own father. And uncle Charles had said so too.

Mr Dedalus covered the dish and began to eat hungrily. Then he said:

– Poor old Christy, he's nearly lopsided now with roguery.

– Simon, said Mrs Dedalus, you haven't given Mrs Riordan any sauce.

Mr Dedalus seized the sauceboat.

– Haven't I? he cried. Mrs Riordan, pity the poor blind.

Dante covered her plate with her hands and said:

– No, thanks.

Mr Dedalus turned to uncle Charles.

– How are you off, sir?

– Right as the mail, Simon.

– You, John?

– I'm all right. Go on yourself.

– Mary? Here, Stephen, here's something to make your hair curl.

He poured sauce freely over Stephen's plate and set the boat again on the table. Then he asked uncle Charles was it tender. Uncle Charles could not speak because his mouth was full; but he nodded that it was.

– That was a good answer our friend made to the canon. What? said Mr Dedalus.

– I didn't think he had that much in him, said Mr Casey.

– *I'll pay your dues, father, when you cease turning the house of God into a polling-booth.*

– A nice answer, said Dante, for any man calling himself a catholic to give to his priest.

– They have only themselves to blame, said Mr

Dedalus suavely. If they took a fool's advice they would confine their attention to religion.

– It is religion, Dante said. They are doing their duty in warning the people.

– We go to the house of God, Mr Casey said, in all humility to pray to our Maker and not to hear election addresses.

– It is religion, Dante said again. They are right. They must direct their flocks.

– And preach politics from the altar, is it? asked Mr Dedalus.

– Certainly, said Dante. It is a question of public morality. A priest would not be a priest if he did not tell his flock what is right and what is wrong.

Mrs Dedalus laid down her knife and fork, saying:

– For pity sake and for pity sake let us have no political discussion on this day of all days in the year.

– Quite right, ma'am, said uncle Charles. Now, Simon, that's quite enough now. Not another word now.

– Yes, yes, said Mr Dedalus quickly.

efore the Paling of the Stars

CHRISTINA ROSSETTI

Before the paling of the stars,
Before the winter morn,
Before the earliest cock crow,
    Jesus Christ was born:
Born in a stable,
    Cradled in a manger,
In the world his hands had made
    Born a stranger.

Priest and king lay fast asleep
    In Jerusalem;
Young and old lay fast asleep
    In crowded Bethlehem:
Saint and angel, ox and ass,
    Kept a watch together
Before the Christmas daybreak
    In the winter weather.

Jesus on his mother's breast
    In the stable cold,
Spotless lamb of God was he,
    Shepherd of the fold:
Let us kneel with Mary maid,
    With Joseph bent and hoary,
With saint and angel, ox and ass,
    To hail the King of Glory.

he Christmas Star

For years and years astronomers have tried to identify the star which, according to the Bible (Matthew 2: 2) led the three wise kings to Bethlehem.

Some think it may have been Halley's Comet, known to have been visible over Bethlehem in 11 BC. Others point to the fact that the orbits of Jupiter, Saturn and Mars were in conjunction in 7 BC or 8 BC, making it seem from earth as if they were one, big, shining star. Or the star of Bethlehem may have been a nova, a star that suddenly becomes extremely brilliant and then, after a short while, fades again into the darkness.

Because the precise date of Christ's birth cannot be established, scientists have been unable to prove any of these theories.

he Twelve Days of Christmas

ANON

The first day of Christmas
My true love sent to me
A partridge in a pear tree.

The second day of Christmas.
My true love sent to me
Two turtle doves, and
A partridge in a pear tree.

The third day of Christmas
My true love sent to me
Three French hens,
Two turtle doves, and
A partridge in a pear tree.

The fourth day of Christmas
My true love sent to me
Four calling birds,
Three French hens,
Two turtle doves, and
A partridge in a pear tree.

The fifth day of Christmas
My true love sent to me
Five gold rings,
Four calling birds,
Three French hens,
Two turtle doves, and
A partridge in a pear tree.

The sixth day of Christmas
My true love sent to me
Six geese a-laying,
Five gold rings,
Four calling birds,
Three French hens,
Two turtle doves, and
A partridge in a pear tree.

The seventh day of Christmas
My true love sent to me
Seven swans a-swimming,
Six geese a-laying,
Five gold rings,
Four calling birds,
Three French hens,
Two turtle doves, and
A partridge in a pear tree.

The eighth day of Christmas
My true love sent to me
Eight maids a-milking,
Seven swans a-swimming,
Six geese a-laying,
Five gold rings,
Four calling birds,
Three French hens,
Two turtle doves, and
A partridge in a pear tree.

The ninth day of Christmas
My true love sent to me
Nine drummers drumming,
Eight maids a-milking,
Seven swans a-swimming,
Six geese a-laying,
Five gold rings,
Four calling birds,
Three French hens,
Two turtle doves, and
A partridge in a pear tree.

The tenth day of Christmas
My true love sent to me
Ten pipers piping,
Nine drummers drumming,
Eight maids a-milking,
Seven swans a-swimming,
Six geese a-laying,
Five gold rings,
Four calling birds,
Three French hens,
Two turtle doves, and
A partridge in a pear tree.

The eleventh day of Christmas
My true love sent to me
Eleven ladies dancing,
Ten pipers piping,
Nine drummers drumming,
Eight maids a-milking,
Seven swans a-swimming,
Six geese a-laying,
Five gold rings,
Four calling birds,
Three French hens,
Two turtle doves, and
A partridge in a pear tree.

The twelfth day of Christmas
My true love sent to me
Twelve lords a-leaping,
Eleven ladies dancing,
Ten pipers piping,
Nine drummers drumming,
Eight maids a-milking,
Seven swans a-swimming,
Six geese a-laying,
Five gold rings,
Four calling birds,
Three French hens,
Two turtle doves, and
A partridge in a pear tree.

ecember Diary

FROM
THE DIARY OF A NOBODY
GEORGE AND WEEDON GROSSMITH

December 19
The annual invitation came to spend with Carrie's mother [Carrie is the wife of the diarist, Mr Pooter] – the usual family festive gathering to which we always look forward. Lupin [grown-up son of the Pooters] declined to go. I was astounded, and expressed my surprise and disgust. Lupin then obliged us with the following Radical speech: 'I hate a family gathering at Christmas. What does it mean? Why, someone says: "Ah! we miss poor Uncle James, who was here last year," and we all begin to snivel. Someone else says, "It's two years since poor Aunt Liz used to sit in that corner." Then we all begin to snivel again. Then another gloomy relation says: "Ah! I wonder whose turn it will be next?" Then we all snivel again, and proceed to eat and drink too much; and they don't discover until *I* get up that we have been seated thirteen at dinner.'

December 20
Went to Smirksons', the drapers, in the Strand, who this year have turned out everything in the shop and devoted the whole place to the sale of Christmas cards. Shop crowded with people, who seemed to take up the cards

rather roughly, and, after a hurried glance at them, throw them down again. I remarked to one of the young persons serving that carelessness appeared to be a disease with some young purchasers. The observation was scarcely out of my mouth when my thick coat-sleeve caught against a huge pile of expensive cards in boxes one on top of the other, and threw them down. The manager came forward, looking very much annoyed, and picking up several cards from the ground, said to one of the assistants, with a palpable side-glance at me: 'Put these amongst the sixpenny goods; they can't be sold for a shilling now.' The result was, I felt it my duty to buy some of these damaged cards.

I had to buy more and pay more than intended. Unfortunately I did not examine them all, and when I got home I discovered a vulgar card with a picture of a fat nurse with two babies, one black and the other white, and the words: 'We wish Pa a Merry Christmas.' I tore up the card and threw it away. Carrie said the great disadvantage of going out in Socoety and increasing the number of our friends was that we should have to send out nearly two dozen cards this year.

December 21
To save the postman a miserable Christmas, we follow the example of all unselfish people and send out our Christmas cards early. Most of the cards had finger-marks, which I did not notice at night. I shall buy all future cards in the daytime. Lupin (who, ever since he has had the appointment with the stock and share broker, does not seem

overscrupulous in his dealings) told me never to rub out the pencilled price on the backs of cards. I asked him why. Lupin said: 'Suppose your card is marked 9d. Well, all you have to do is to pencil a 3 – and a long down-stroke after it – in *front* of the ninepence, and people will think you have given five times the price for it.'

In the evening Lupin was very low-spirited, and I reminded him that behind the clouds the sun was shining. He said: 'Ugh! it never shines on me.' I said: 'Stop, Lupin, my boy; you are worried about Daisy Mutlar [Lupin's former fiancée]. Don't think about her any more. You ought to congratulate yourself on having got off a very bad bargain. Her notions are far too grand for our simple tastes.' He jumped up and said: 'I won't allow one word to be uttered against her. She's worth the whole bunch of your friends put together, that inflated sloping-head of Perkupp included.' I left the room with silent dignity but caught my foot in the mat.

ongs in Season

Christmas-Tide
St Thomas's Day is past and gone,
And Christmas almost come,
Maidens arise,
And make your pies,
And save young Bobby some.

Christmas is coming,
The geese are getting fat,
Please to put a penny
In the old man's hat.
If you haven't got a penny,
A ha'penny will do;
If you haven't got a ha'penny,
Then God bless you!

Christmas comes but once a year,
And when it comes it brings good cheer,
A pocket full of money, and a cellar full of beer.

God bless the master of this house,
And its good mistress too,
And all the little children
That round the table go;
And all your kin and kinsmen,
That dwell both far and near;
We wish you a merry Christmas
And a happy New Year.

 *now Pancakes*

These are fun, seasonal and very tasty light pale pancakes. Very easy to make, too.

Beat together a pint and a half of milk (350 ml) and just over 1 lb (half kilo) of plain flour. Add three-quarters of a pound of fresh, light snow. Put the mixture aside for a couple of hours to allow the snow to melt and aerate the flour and milk. Then cook as you would any pancake.

If you prefer them richer, simply add a few egg yokes.

he Season Of Light

ÉAMON KELLY

As well as pattern day there is one other religious observance of long ago worth recalling. I'm thinking of Christmas. No word of a lie but it was something to write home about when I was small. Oh! the way we looked forward to twilight on Christmas Eve, for when darkness fell it was Christmas Night, the greatest night of all the year. We youngsters would be up with the crack of dawn that morning to have the house ready for the night.

Berry holly would have to be cut and brought in to deck out the windows, the top of the dresser, the back of the settle and the clevvy. We'd bring in ivy too and put a sprig of laurel behind the pictures, above the lintel of the door and around the fireplace. But we wouldn't overdo it, or if we did my mother would make us cut it down a bit, reminding us that she'd like to feel that she was in her own house for Christmas, and not in the middle of a wood!

Well, the transformation we could bring about in the kitchen with all that greenery! But we weren't finished yet. The Christmas candles had to be prepared; these were of white tallow as thick as the handle of a spade and nearly as tall. In some houses they'd scoop out a hole in a turnip and put the candle sitting into it. A big crock we'd use.

We'd put the candle standing into that and pack it around with sand. If you hadn't sand, bran or pollard would do.

When the candle was firm in position we'd spike sprigs of holly or laurel into the sand about the candle, and we had coloured paper too to put around the outside of the crock to take the bare look off it. With that same coloured paper, the girls in the family, if they were anyway handy, could make paper flowers to decorate the holly. Then what would cap it all, was a length of young ivy and spiral it up around the candle – it looked lovely! That done, we would go through the same manoeuvre until there was a candle in a crock for every window in the house.

Then we'd be praying for night to fall, for you couldn't see the right effect until the candles were lit. That honour would fall to the youngest in the house. My father would lift him up saying: 'In the name of the Father and of the son . . . ' and when the child had blessed himself, he would put the lighting spill to the candle, and from that candle the other candles would be lit, and we'd be half daft with excitement, enjoying the great blaze of light, and running from the rooms to the kitchen and out into the yard to see what the effect was like from the outside. When we'd get tired of looking at the candles in our own windows, we'd turn and try to name the neighbours' houses as the bunches of lights came on, two windows here and three windows there, across the dark countryside and away up to the foot of the hills. And as sure as anything someone'd be late and we'd rush into my mother saying:

'Faith, then, there's no light on yet in Rosacrew!'

'Go on yeer knees!' my mother would say. The time

she'd pick for the Rosary, just as the salt ling was ready and the white onion sauce and the potatoes steaming over the fire. But I suppose there'd be no religion in the world only for the women. The Rosary in our house didn't end at five decades. Not at all. After the Hail Holy Queen my mother would branch into the Trimmings:

> Come Holy Ghost send down those beams,
> Which sweetly flow in silent streams.

She'd pray for everyone in sickness and in need: the poor souls and the sinful soul that was at that very moment trembling before the Judgement seat above. She'd pray for the sailor on the seas: 'Protect him from the tempest, Oh Lord, and bring him safely home.' And the lone traveller on the highway and of course our emigrants and, last of all, the members of her own family:

> God bless and save us all
> St Patrick, Bridget and Colmcille
> Guard each wall.
> May the Queen of heaven
> And the angels bright
> Keep us and our house
> From all harm this night!

Our knees'd be aching as we got up off the floor, and it would take my father a while to get the prayer arch out of his back. Well, we wouldn't be sitting down to the supper when my mother'd bless herself again, a preliminary to grace before meals, and you could hardly blame my father for losing his patience.

'Is it in a monastery we are?' he'd say. 'Haven't we done enough praying for one night?'

After the supper there was Christmas cake for anyone with a sweet tooth. My father'd never look at that. His eye'd be on the big earthenware jar below the dresser, and it would be a great relief to him when my mother'd say to us:

'Go out there, one of ye, and tell the neighbouring men to come in for a while.'

It was the custom that night, *Nollaig Mhor*, big Christmas, for the men to visit each other's houses. The women were too busy to be bothered. They had their own night, *Nollaig na mBan*, small Christmas, for making tapes. In a while's time the men'd come, and at the first lag in the conversation my father'd take the cork off the jar and fill out a few cups of porter. The men, by the way, not noticing what was going on, and then when they'd get the cups, all surprise they'd say:

'What's this? What's this for?'

'Go on take it,' my father'd say. 'It is Christmas night, neighbours, and more luck to us!'

Then the men's faces'd light up and lifting their cups they'd say:

'Happy Christmas, Ned. Happy Christmas, Hannie. Happy Christmas, everyone!'

'And the same to ye men,' my father would answer. 'May we all be alive again this time twelve months.'

And my mother, who was never very happy in the

presence of strong drink, would direct her gaze in the direction of the Christmas candle and say:
'The grace of God to us all!'
After sampling the beverage one of the men, putting out his lower lip to suck in any stray particles of froth that had lodged in his moustache, would inquire: 'Where did you get this, Ned?'
'Carthy Dannehy's', my father'd say.
'He always keeps a good drop, I'll say that for him.'
'*Sláinte*, Ned,' from all the men.

    Sláinte chugat is cabhair
    Dealbh go deo ná rabhair,
    Is go bhfásfaidh gach ribín
    Ar do cheann chomh fada le meigeal ghabhair.

from *The Rub of a Relic*

 hristmas at Sea

ROBERT LOUIS STEVENSON

The sheets were frozen hard, and they cut the naked hand;
The decks were like a slide, where a seaman scarce could stand,
The wind was a nor'-wester, blowing squally off the sea;
And cliffs and spouting breakers were the only things a-lee.

They heard the surf a-roaring before the break of day;
But 'twas only with the peep of the light we saw how ill we lay.
We tumbled every hand on deck instanter, with a shout,
And we gave her the maintops'l, and stood by to go about.

All day we tack'd and tack'd between the South Head and the North;
All day we haul'd the frozen sheets, and got no further forth;
All day as cold as charity, in bitter pain and dread,
For very life and nature we tack'd from head to head.

We gave the South a wider berth, for there the tide-race
    roar'd;
But every tack we made we brought the North Head
    close abroad;
So's we saw the cliffs and houses, and the breakers
    running high,
And the coastguard in his garden, with his glass against
    his eye.

The frost was on the village roofs as white as ocean
    foam;
The good red fires were burning bright in every
    'longshore home;
The windows sparkled clear, and the chimneys volley'd
    out;
And I vow we sniff'd the victuals as the vessel went
    about.

The bells upon the church were rung with a mighty
    jovial cheer;
For it's just that I should tell you how (of all days in
    the year)
This day of our adversity was blessèd Christmas morn,
And the house above the coastguard's was the house
    where I was born.

O well I saw the pleasant room, the pleasant faces
    there,
My mother's silver spectacles, my father's silver hair;

And well I saw the firelight, like a flight of homely elves
Go dancing round the china-plates that stand upon the shelves!

And well I knew the talk they had, the talk that was of me,
Of the shadow on the household and the son that went to sea;
And O the wicked fool I seem'd, in every kind of way,
To be here and hauling frozen on blessèd Christmas Day.

They lit the high sea-light, and the dark began to fall.
'All hands to loose topgallant sails!' I heard the captain call.
'By the Lord, she'll never stand it,' our first mate Jackson cried.
. . . 'it's the one way or the other, Mr Jackson,' he replied.

She stagger'd to her bearings, but the sails were new and good,
And the ship smelt up to windward just as though she understood.
As the winter's day was ending, in the entry of the night,
We clear'd the weary headland, and pass'd below the light.

And they heaved a mighty breath, every soul on board but me,
As they saw her nose again pointing handsome out to sea;
But all that I could think of, in the darkness and the cold,
Was just that I was leaving home and my folks were growing old.

 olly and Ivy and all that Greenery

Long before the birth of Christ, evergreens were used for decorative and ceremonial purposes by the Romans. During their winter festival, called the Saturnalia, they carried laurel, holly, and other greens in procession as well as decorating their homes and temples with garlands and flowers.

The kiss beneath the mistletoe comes from the Roman belief that the plant was a symbol of peace and that enemies could be reconciled by meeting beneath it.

The use of holly, however, is purely Christian in origin. It is said to symbolise Christ's crown of thorns – the pointy leaves are his wounds and the red berries his blood.

# hristmas with the Savages

MARY CLIVE

As soon as we got into Lady Tamerlane's sitting-room there was a scurry for the alcove and the glass doors. Ourselves in deep shadow, we looked through into the ballroom, which was blazing with light from dozens of candles. In the middle stood an immense Christmas tree, glittering, sparkling, dazzling.

'O-o-ooh!' we all said.

My memory of the rest of the evening is rather confused. I can see us joining hands and dancing round the tree, and I can see Mr O'Sullivan walking about with a sponge on the end of a long stick with which he put out any dangerous candles, and I can see a work-basket lined with red satin which I suppose was my present, and I can see the fairy doll at the top which I wanted but didn't get – no-one got it – and I can see the servants crowding in at a side-door and coming up one by one to receive a roll of dark cloth from Lady Tamerlane – each bobbed low as she took her roll and then the next one came forward.

And then somehow we were upstairs again in the twilight of our bedrooms eating our suppers and chattering. We all had a glass of milk, and a ginger biscuit and a marie biscuit, which could either be eaten one at a time or together like a sandwich. Both ways made a lot of crumbs.

Peggy ran into my room to swap her marie for my ginger and I ran into hers to borrow a big safety-pin (you can probably guess what for). Marguerite had remembered to pack one of my father's stockings but not a safety-pin. However, Nana Glen had quantities of them, and my brass bed-rail was just the shape I needed.

Then I heard the Savages giggling so much that I had to run into their room to see what was happening. Harry had fallen out of bed and Nana Savage had said, 'Get back to bed, you silly little fellow,' but he continued to lie on the floor, laughing and unable to move. The nurses were all rather keen to hurry us along, as later in the evening there was to be dancing. (In the housekeeper's room the music was provided by Mr O'Sullivan who played the violin, and in the servants' hall there was a sort of barrel organ.)

But, before that, mothers had to come round to hear prayers and say good-night. As I hadn't a mother Lady Tamerlane heard my prayers, which she did in the brisk business-like way that she did everything. She carried a special candlestick with a glass funnel to protect the flame as she moved swiftly down the corridor, and she went round the children and kissed them in turn.

Then our own candles were blown out and we were left lying in the dark to wait for Father Christmas. We were all excited but in different ways, from Tommy who was so horrified and revolted by the idea of a dreadful old man coming down the chimney in the middle of the night that they had had to hand his stocking outside his door, to

Lionel who had put a wet sponge beside his bed with the worst intentions. I was in that state when you don't know what to expect or whom to believe, and I several times crept to the end of my bed to feel my limp stocking. Was it possible that in a few hours' time that dingy woollen object would be oozing toys?

Just as I was dropping off to sleep I was roused by the sound of the Savages' door being violently thrown open and bare feet pattering along the passage.

'Nana!' wailed Harry, 'Minnie! May! *My stocking's empty! There's nothing in it!*'

Loud unfeeling laughter burst from the nursery and presently Harry was led back to bed by Minnie, who explained gently that though he had been asleep, it wasn't morning.

I was glad Harry had made such a disturbance as I had been getting very drowsy myself and I did really mean to lie awake till Father Christmas came so as to settle once and for all *who* he was. But the room was pitch dark except for a strip of light under the door, and it was very difficult to keep my eyes open. I could see the pictures of stags but I wondered what they would think of reindeer. 'Is Father Christmas a Cavalier or a Roundhead? And suppose he has hooks instead of hands, and hooks instead of feet, and wears a pink sash . . . '

Christmas Day
Presently I noticed that the crack of light wasn't there any more, and as I lay in the dark I became aware of a strong smell of oranges. Vaguely I wondered where the smell was

coming from and then, with a start, I asked myself, could it be coming from my stocking?

Regardless of the cold, I pushed back the bedclothes and crawled to the end of my bed and my hand met something that was woolly, hard and sharp. Nothing else in the world feels quite like a well-stuffed stocking.

My hand followed the bumps and jags up to the top and there the woolliness ended and I could feel something which in the darkness I mistook for the top of an umbrella – it afterwards turned out to be a book. With a sigh of relief I nipped back under the bedclothes thinking, 'The Magic has worked yet once again. He has come.'

Oíche Nollag

MÁIRE MHAC AN TSAOI

Le coinnle na n-aingeal tá an spéir amuigh breactha,
Tá fiacail an tseaca sa ghaoith ón gcnoc,
Adaigh an tine is téir chun na leapan,
Luífidh Mac Dé ins an tigh seo anocht.

Fágaidh an doras ar leathadh ina coinne,
An mhaighdean a thiocfaidh is a naí ar a hucht,
Deonaigh scíth an bhóthair a ligint, a Mhuire,
Luíodh Mac Dé ins an tigh seo anocht.

Bhí soilse ar lasadh i dtigh sin na haíochta,
Cóiriú gan caoile, bia agus deoch,
Do cheannaithe olla, do cheannaithe síoda,
Ach luífidh Mac Dé ins an tigh seo anocht.

 *he Christmas Tree*

We can't be certain, but it seems likely that the Christmas tree began life in Germany in the Middle Ages. The evergreen was seen as a symbol of immortality and of the Christian spirit. By the eighteenth. century the people of many other Christian countries across Europe had taken to decorated trees both in and outside their houses.

But the roots of the tradition go back a lot further, to the pagan peoples who worshipped trees and nature. It was St Boniface, the English missionary who brought Christianity to Germany in the eighth century, who substituted the evergreen for the oak which people had been used to worship at the mid-winter festival.

Tinsel is said to have begun with a poor woman who decorated a tree only to have spiders cover it with webs during the night. The Christ Child, realising that the woman's surprise for her family would be spoiled, turned the spider webs into silver.

ast Bus for Christmas

PATRICIA LYNCH

'Hurry up there, Miheal! Will ye bring over two red candles quick!'

'More strawberry jam, Miheal! Two one-pound jars! And raisins: four one-pound bags!'

'Miheal Daly! I'm wore out wid waitin' for twine. How can I parcel the customers' groceries wid ne'er an inch of string?'

Miheal grabbed a handful of string from the box in the corner behind the biscuit tins and ran with it to Mr Coughlan. He brought the jam and the raisins at the same time to Peter Cadogan, and rolled the candles along the counter to Jim Reardon. Then he went back to his job of filling half-pound bags with sugar.

Miheal was shop-boy and, one day, if he worked hard and behaved himself, Mr Coughlan had promised to make him an assistant.

'There's grandeur for an orphan!' Mrs Coughlan told him. 'Ye should be grateful.'

Miheal was grateful. But, as he watched the women crowding the other side of the counter, filling market bags and baskets with Christmas shopping, he was discontented. Yet he had whistled and sung as he put up the coloured paper chains and decorated the window with yards of tinsel and artificial holly.

He nibbled a raisin and gazed out at the sleet drifting past the open door.

Everybody's going home for Christmas but me, he thought.

The Coughlans always went to their relations for Christmas. Mrs Coughlan left Miheal plenty to eat and Mr Coughlan gave him a shilling to spend. But Miheal never ate his Christmas dinner until they came back. After Mass he spent Christmas Day walking about the streets, listening to the noise and clatter that came from the houses.

'Only two more hours,' whispered Peter Cadogan, as Miheal brought him bags of biscuits and half-pounds of rashers as fast as Mr Coughlan could cut them.

'Two more sugars, Miheal,' said Jim Reardon. 'Where d'you get your bus?'

Jim was new. He didn't know Miheal was an orphan, and Miheal was ashamed to tell him he had no home to go to for Christmas.

'Aston's Quay,' he muttered.

'We'll go together,' said Jim over his shoulder. 'I've me bag under the counter. Get yours!'

The next time Miheal brought Jim candles and raisins the new assistant wanted to know what time Miheal's bus went.

'I'll just make it if I run,' said Miheal.

'Then get yer bag, lad. Get yer bag!'

Miheal slipped through the door leading to the house. He ran to his little dark room under the stairs. He didn't dare switch on the light. Mrs Coughlan would want to know what he was doing. And a nice fool he'd look if she found out he was pretending to go home for Christmas.

'Home!' said Miheal to himself. 'That's where a lad's people come from and mine came from Carrigasheen.'

He wrapped his few belongings in an old waterproof. He grabbed his overcoat from the hook behind the door and was back in the shop before Mr Coughlan could miss him.

'Hi, Miheal! Give me a hand with this side of bacon. I never cut so many rashers in me life!'

Miheal pushed his bundle under the counter and ran to help.

'Isn't it grand to be going home for Christmas!' cried Peter, as they closed the door to prevent any more customers from coming in.

'Isn't it terrible to be turning money away!' groaned Mr Coughlan.

But Mrs Coughlan was waiting for him in her best hat and the coat with the fur collar.

'Can I trust you lads to bolt the shop door an' let yerselves out be the side door?' demanded Mr Coughlan.

'Indeed you can, sir!' replied Peter and Jim.

The last customer was served.

'I'm off!' cried Peter.

'Safe home!' called the others.

Then Jim was running down the quay, Miheal stumbling after him, clasping his bundle, his unbuttoned coat flapping in the wind.

They went along Burgh Quay, pushing by the people waiting for the Bray bus, then across to Aston's Quay.

'There's me bus!' shouted Jim.

"'Tis packed full!' murmured Miheal. He was terribly sorry for Jim. But maybe he'd come back with him and they could spend Christmas together.

The bus was moving.

Jim gave a leap, the conductor caught his arm and pulled him to safety. He turned and waved to Miheal, his round red face laughing. He would have to stand all the way, but Jim was used to standing.

Two queues still waited. Miheal joined the longest.

'Where are ye bound for, avic?' asked a stout country-woman, with a thin little girl and four large bundles, who came up after him.

'Carrigasheen!' replied Miheal proudly.

'Ah, well! I never heard tell of the place. But no doubt ye'll be welcome when ye get there. An' here's the bus.'

'I'll help with the bundles, ma'am,' said Miheal politely.

Now every seat was filled. Still more people squeezed into the bus. Miheal reached the step.

'One more, an' one more only!' announced the conductor. 'In ye go, ma'am!' said Miheal, stepping back.

The little girl was in. Miheal pushed the bundles after her and everyone cried out when the conductor tried to keep back the stout woman.

'Sure ye can't take the child away from her mammy!' declared a thin man. 'Haven't ye any Christianity in yer bones?'

'Can't she sit on me lap?' demanded the stout woman. 'Give me a h'ist up, lad. And God reward ye!' she added, turning to Miheal.

He seized her under the arms. She caught the shining

rail and Miheal gave a great heave.

He stood gazing after the bus.

'Now, I'm stranded!' he said, forgetting he had no need to leave Dublin.

A dash of sleet in Miheal's face reminded him. He could go back to the lonely house behind the shop. His supper would be waiting on the table in the kitchen. He could poke up the fire and read his library book.

The quays were deserted. A tall garda strolled along. He stared curiously at Miheal and his bundle.

'Missed the bus, lad?' he asked.

''Twas full up,' explained Miheal.

'Bad luck!' sympathised the garda. 'Can ye go back where ye came from?'

Miheal nodded.

''Tis a bad night to be travelling!' said the garda. 'That's the way to look at it.'

He gave Miheal a friendly nod and passed on.

I'd as well be getting me supper, thought Miheal.

But he did not move.

Over the Metal Bridge came a queer old coach drawn by two horses. The driver was wrapped in a huge coat with many capes and a broad-brimmed hat was pulled down over his twinkling eyes.

He flourished a whip and pulled up beside Miheal.

The boy edged away. He didn't like the look of the coach at all.

The driver leaned over and managed to open the door at the back with his whip.

'In ye get! Last bus for Christmas!'

Whoever saw a bus with horses! thought Miheal. But I suppose they use any old traps at Christmas.

Still he held back.

'All the way to Carrigasheen widout stoppin!' said the driver.

Miheal could see the cushioned seats and the floor spread thick with fresh hay. The wind, which was growing fiercer and colder every moment, blew in his face. He gave one look along the desolate quay and, putting his foot on the iron step, scrambled in.

At once the door slammed shut. The driver gave a shout and the horses trotted over the stones.

The coach bumped and swayed. Miheal tried to stretch out on the seat, but he slipped to the floor. The hay was thick and clean. He put his bundle under his head for a pillow and fell asleep.

An extra bump woke him up.

'I never thought to ask the fare,' said Miheal to himself. 'Seems a long way, so it does. Would he want ten shillings? He might – easy! Well, I haven't ten shillings. I've two new half-crowns. He'll get one and not a penny more!'

He tried to stand up, the coach was swaying from side to side and he had to sit down again.

'Mister! Mister!' he shouted. 'How much is the fare?'

The rattling of the coach and the thunder of the horses' hooves made so much noise he could scarcely hear himself. Yet he would not keep quiet.

'I won't pay a penny more than two and six,' he shouted. 'Mind now! I'm telling you.'

The door of the coach swung open and Miheal was

pitched out, his bundle following him. He landed on a bank covered with snow and lay there blinking.

The road wound away through the mountains in the moonlight – an empty desolate road. The wind had dropped but snow was falling.

In the distance he could hear a strange sound. It was coming nearer and nearer, and soon Miheal knew it was someone singing 'Adeste Fideles' in a queer cracked voice.

The singer approached, tramping slowly along: an old man with a heavy sack on his back.

'What ails ye to be sitting there in the snow, at this late hour of the night, young lad?' he asked, letting his sack slip to the ground.

'I came on the coach from Dublin,' replied Miheal, standing up.

He was ashamed to say he had fallen out.

The old man pushed back his battered caubeen and scratched his head.

'But there hasn't been a coach on this road in mortal memory!' he declared. 'There's the bus road the other side of the mountain and the last bus went by nigh on two hours ago. I suppose ye came by that. Where are ye bound for?'

'Mebbe I did come by the bus and mebbe I didn't!' exclaimed Miheal. 'But I'd be thankful if you'd tell me am I right for Carrigasheen?'

The old man wasn't a bit annoyed by Miheal's crossness.

'D'ye see the clump of trees where the road bends round by the mountain. There's Carrigasheen! I'm on me way there an' I'll be real glad of company. So ye're home for Christmas? I thought I knew everyone for miles around, yet I don't remember yer face. What name is on ye, lad?'

'Miheal Daly.'

The old man stared.

'There are no Dalys in Carrigasheen now. That I do know! But we can talk as we go. Me own name is Paudeen Caffrey.'

Miheal caught up the sack. He was a strong lad but he found it heavy. He wondered how the old man had managed to carry it at all. Paudeen Caffrey took the boy's bundle and they set off. The snow piled on their shoulders, on the loads they carried, on their hair, their eyebrows, but they did not notice, for Miheal was telling the old man all about himself.

'So me poor gossoon, ye're an orphan,' asked the old man.

'I am indeed!' agreed Miheal.

'An' ye haven't a father or mother, or brother or sister to be a friend to ye?'

'Not a soul!'

'An' these people ye work for, what class of people are they?' continued old Paudeen Caffrey.

'Not too bad!' declared Miheal. 'Aren't they going to make me an assistant one of these days?'

'Suppose now,' began the old man. 'Mind, I'm just saying suppose – ye have a chance to be shop-boy to an old man and his wife that needed help bad in their shop and couldn't get it? Mind ye – I'm only supposing. Ye'd have a room wid two windas, one lookin' out on the market square, the other at the mountains. Ye'd have three good meals a day, a snack at supper, ten shillings a week, an' if ye wanted to keep a dog or a cat, or a bicycle, ye'd be welcome. What would ye say to that?'

He looked at Miheal sideways and Miheal looked back.

'It wouldn't be with Paudeen Caffrey, that kept the corner shop next the post office, would it? asked Miheal.

'It would so,' replied the old man.

'I'm remembering now,' said the boy. 'Me father told me if ever I needed a friend to write to Paudeen Caffrey.'

'Why didn't ye, lad? Why didn't ye?'

'I was ashamed. Me mother told me how they left Carrigasheen after telling everyone they were going to Dublin to make their fortunes an', when they came back, they'd be riding in their carriage. Ye see?'

The old man laughed.

'An' didn't ye come back in a carriage? But there's the lights of Carrigasheen. Do ye come home wid me, Miheal Daly?'

'If you'll have me, Mr Caffrey.'

'The old man chuckled.

'An' to think I went out for a sack of praties an' come back wid a shop-boy! Wasn't it well ye caught the last bus for Christmas, Miheal?'

'It was indeed!' declared Miheal Daly.

He could see the corner shop with the door open and an old woman looking out. Beyond her he caught a glimpse of firelight dancing on the walls, of holy pictures framed in holly and a big red Christmas candle on the table waiting for the youngest in the house to light it.

Once in Royal David's City

CECIL FRANCES ALEXANDER

Once in Royal David's City
Stood a lonely cattle shed,
Where a Mother laid her Baby
In a manger for His bed;
Mary was that Mother mild,
Jesus Christ her little child.

He came down to earth from Heaven
Who is God and Lord of all,
And his shelter was a stable,
And his cradle was a stall;
With the poor, and mean, and lowly,
Lived on earth our Saviour Holy.

And through all His wondrous Childhood,
He would honour and obey,
Love, and watch the lowly Maiden,
In whose gentle arms He lay;
Christian children all must be
Mild, obedient, good as He.

For He is our childhood's pattern,
Day by day like us he grew.
He was little, weak, and helpless,
Tears and smile like us he knew
And He feeleth for our sadness,
And He shareth in our gladness.

And our eyes at last shall see Him,
Through His own redeeming love,
For that Child so dear and gentle
Is our Lord in Heav'n above;
And He leads His children on
To the place where He is gone.

Not in that poor lowly stable,
With the oxen standing by,
We shall see Him; but in Heaven,
Set at God's right hand on high;
When like stars His children crown'd
All in white shall wait around.

 # hristmas Candles

Christmas candles are said to be symbolic of Christ, 'the light of the world'. The practice of putting a candle in the window on Christmas Eve, especially widespread in Ireland, began in the Middle Ages. The idea then, and for a long time, was to guide the Christchild to Christian homes. It was also a sign to travellers and pilgrims that they could expect a welcome in homes burning a candle.

The Twelve Days Of Christmas

A CORRESPONDENCE

JOHN JULIUS NORWICH

25th December

My dearest darling
That partridge, in that lovely little pear tree! What an enchanting, romantic, poetic present! Bless you and thank you.
Your deeply loving Emily

26th December

My dearest darling Edward
The two turtle doves arrived this morning and are cooing away in the pear tree as I write. I'm so touched and grateful.
With undying love, as always, Emily

27th December

My darling Edward
You do think of the most original presents, whoever thought of sending anybody three French hens? Do they really come all the way from France? It's a pity that we have no chicken coops, but I expect we'll find some. Thank you, anyway, they're lovely.
Your loving Emily

> 28th December

Dearest Edward

What a surprise – four calling birds arrived this morning. They are very sweet, even if they do call rather loudly – they make telephoning impossible. But I expect they'll calm down when they get used to their new home. Anyway, I'm very grateful – of course I am.

Love from Emily

> 29th December

Dearest Edward

The postman has just delivered five most beautiful gold rings, one for each finger, and all fitting perfectly. A really lovely present – lovelier in a way than birds, which do take rather a lot of looking after. The four that arrived yesterday are still making a terrible row, and I'm afraid none of us got much sleep last night. Mummy says she wants to use the rings to 'wring' their necks – she's only joking, I think; though I know what she means. But I *love* the rings. Bless you.

Love, Emily

> 30th December

Dear Edward

Whatever I expected to find when I opened the front door this morning, it certainly wasn't six socking great geese laying eggs all over the doorstep. Frankly, I rather hoped you had stopped sending me birds – we have no room for them and they have already ruined the croquet lawn. I know you meant well, but – let's call a halt, shall we?

Love, Emily

31st December

Edward

I thought I said no more birds; but this morning I woke up to find no less than seven swans all trying to get into our tiny goldfish pond. I'd rather not think what happened to the goldfish. The whole house seems to be full of birds – to say nothing of what they leave behind them. Please, please stop.

Your Emily

1st January

Frankly, I think I prefer the birds. What am I to do with eight milkmaids – And their cows? Is this some kind of a joke? If so, I'm afraid I don't find it very amusing.

Emily

2nd January

Look here Edward, this has gone far enough. You say you're sending me nine ladies dancing; all I can say is that judging from the way they dance, they're certainly not ladies. The village just isn't accustomed to seeing a regiment of shameless hussies with nothing on but their lipstick cavorting round the green – and it's Mummy and I who get blamed. If you value our friendship – which I do less and less – kindly stop this ridiculous behaviour at once.

Emily

3rd January

As I write this letter, ten disgusting old men are prancing about all over what used to be the garden – before the geese

and the swans and the cows got at it; and several of them, I notice, are taking inexcusable liberties with the milkmaids. Meanwhile the neighbours are trying to have us evicted. I shall never speak to you again.
Emily

                                                                      4th January

This is the last straw. You know I detest bagpipes. The place has now become something between a menagerie and a madhouse and a man from the Council has just declared it unfit for habitation. At least Mummy has been spared this last outrage; they took her away yesterday afternoon in an ambulance. I hope you're satisfied.

                                                                       5th January

Sir

Our client, Miss Emily Wilbraham, instructs me to inform you that with the arrival on her premises at half-past seven this morning of the entire percussion section of the Liverpool Philharmonic Orchestra and several of their friends she has no course left open to her but to seek an injunction to prevent your importuning her further. I am making arrangements for the return of much assorted livestock.

I am, Sir, Yours faithfully,
G. Creep
Solicitor-at-Law

# The Christmas Stocking

This is another tradition for which we have St Nicholas to thank. The story goes that the good bishop, having heard of the plight of three sisters who were unable to marry for lack of dowries, decided to help them. So as each sister reached marriageable age, he tossed a bag of gold through her window. One of these landed in a stocking which had been hung near the fire to dry. Ever hopeful, people thereafter began to hang up stockings for St Nicholas to fill with gifts.

Scrooge's Christmas Day

FROM
A CHRISTMAS CAROL
CHARLES DICKENS

Yes! and the bedpost was his own. The bed was his own, the room was his own. Best and happiest of all, the Time before him was his own, to make amends in!

'I will live in the Past, the Present, and the Future!' Scrooge repeated, as he scrambled out of bed. 'The Spirits of all Three shall strive within me. Oh Jacob Marley! Heaven, and the Christmas Time be praised for this! I say it on my knees, old Jacob, on my knees!'

He was so fluttered and so glowing with his good intentions, that his broken voice would scarcely answer to his call. He had been sobbing violently in his conflict with the Spirit, and his face was wet with tears.

'They are not torn down,' cried Scrooge, folding one of his bed-curtains in his arms, 'they are not torn down, rings and all. They are here – I am here – shadows of the things that would have been, may be dispelled. They will be. I know they will!'

His hands were busy with his garments all this time; turning them inside out, putting them on upside down, tearing them, mislaying them, making them parties to every kind of extravagance.

'I don't know what to do!' cried Scrooge, laughing and crying in the same breath; and making a perfect Laocoon of himself with his stockings. 'I am as light as a feather, I am as happy as an angel, I am as merry as a schoolboy. I am as giddy as a drunken man. A merry Christmas to everybody! A happy New Year to all the world! Hallo here! Whoop! Hallo!'

He had frisked into the sitting-room, and was now standing there: perfectly winded.

'There's the saucepan that the gruel was in!' cried Scrooge, starting off again, and going round the fireplace. 'There's the door, by which the Ghost of Jacob Marley entered! There's the corner where the Ghost of Christmas Present, sat! There's the window where I saw the wandering Spirits! It's all right, it's all true, it all happened. Ha, ha, ha!'

Really, for a man who had been out of practice for so many years, it was a splendid laugh, a most illustrious laugh. The father of a long, long line of brilliant laughs!

'I don't know what day of the month it is!' said Scrooge. 'I don't know how long I've been among the Spirits. I don't know anything. I'm quite a baby. Never mind. I don't care. I'd rather be a baby. Hallo! Whoop! Hallo here!'

He was checked in his transports by the churches ringing out the lustiest peals he had ever heard. Clash, clang, hammer; ding, dong, bell. Bell, dong, ding; hammer, clang, clash! Oh, glorious, glorious!

Running to the window, he opened it, and put out his

head. No fog, no mist; clear, bright, jovial stirring, cold; cold, piping for the blood to dance to; Golden sunlight; Heavenly sky; sweet fresh air; merry bells. Oh, glorious! Glorious!

'What's to-day?' cried Scrooge, calling downward to a boy in Sunday clothes, who perhaps had loitered in to look about him.

'Eh?' returned the boy, with all his might of wonder.

'What's to-day, my fine fellow?' said Scrooge.

'To-day!' replied the boy. 'Why, Christmas Day.'

'It's Christmas Day!' said Scrooge to himself. 'I haven't missed it. The Spirits have done it all in one night. They can do anything they like. Of course they can. Of course they can. Hallo, my fine fellow!'

'Hallo!' returned the boy.

'Do you know the Poulterer's, in the next street but one at the corner?' Scrooge inquired.

'I should hope I did,' replied the lad.

'An intelligent boy!' said Scrooge. 'A remarkable boy! Do you know whether they've sold the prize Turkey that was hanging up there? – Not the little prize Turkey: the big one?'

'What, the one as big as me?' returned the boy.

'What a delightful boy!' said Scrooge. 'It's a pleasure to talk to him. Yes, my buck!'

'It's hanging there now,' replied the boy.

'Is is?' said Scrooge. 'Go and buy it.'

'Walk-ER!' exclaimed the boy.

'No, no,' said Scrooge, 'I am in earnest. Go and buy it, and tell 'em to bring it here, that I may give them the direction where to take it. Come back with the man, and I'll give you a shilling. Come back with him in less than five minutes and I'll give you half-a-crown!'

The boy was off like a shot. He must have had a steady hand at a trigger who could have got a shot off half so fast.

'I'll send it to Bob Cratchit's!' whispered Scrooge, rubbing his hands, and splitting with a laugh. 'He sha'n't know who sends it. It's twice the size of Tiny Tim. Joe Miller never made such a joke as sending it to Bob's will be!'

The hand in which he wrote the address was not a steady one, but write it he did, somehow, and went downstairs to open the street door, for the coming of the poulterer's man. As he stood there, waiting his arrival, the knocker caught his eye.

'I shall love it, as long as I live!' cried Scrooge, patting it with his hand. 'I scarcely ever looked at it before. What an honest expression it has in its face! It's a wonderful knocker! – Here's the Turkey. Hallo! Whoop! How are you! Merry Christmas!'

It *was* a Turkey! He never could have stood upon his legs, that bird. He would have snapped 'em short off in a minute, like stocks of sealing-wax.

'Why, it's impossible to carry to Camden Town,' said Scrooge. 'You must have a cab.'

The chuckle with which he said this, and the chuckle with which he paid for the Turkey, and the chuckle with which he paid for the cab, and the chuckle with which he recompensed the boy, were only to be exceeded by the chuckle with which he sat down breathless in his chair again, and chuckled till he cried.

Shaving was not an easy task, for his hand continued to shake very much; and shaving required attention, even when you don't dance while you are at it. But had he cut the end of his nose off, he would have put a piece of sticking-plaister over it, and been quite satisfied.

He dressed himself 'all in his best', and at last got out into the streets. The people were by this time pouring forth, as he had seen them with the Ghost of Christmas Present; and walking with his hands behind him, Scrooge regarded every one with a delighted smile. He looked so irresistibly pleasant, in a word, that three or four good-humoured fellows said, 'Good morning, sir! A merry Christmas to you!' and Scrooge said often afterwards, that of all the blithe sounds he had ever heard, those were the blithest in his ears.

He had not gone far, when coming on towards him he beheld the portly gentleman, who had walked into his counting-house the day before, and said, 'Scrooge and Marley's, I believe?' It sent a pang across his heart to think how this old gentleman would look upon him when they met; but he knew what path lay straight before him, and he took it.

'My dear sir,' said Scrooge, quickening his pace, and taking the old gentleman by both his hands. 'How do you do? I hope you succeeded yesterday. It was very kind of you. A merry Christmas to you, sir!'

'Mr Scrooge?'

'Yes,' said Scrooge. 'That is my name, and I fear it may

not be pleasant to you. Allow me to ask your pardon. And will you have the goodness' – here Scrooge whispered in his ear.

'Lord bless me!' cried the gentleman, as if his breath were taken away. 'My dear Mr Scrooge, are you serious?'

'If you please,' said Scrooge. 'Not a farthing less. A great many back-payments are included in it, I assure you. Will you do me that favour?'

'My dear sir,' said the other, shaking hands with him. 'I don't know what to say to such munifi – '

'Don't say anything, please,' retorted Scrooge. 'Come and see me. Will you come and see me?'

'I will!' cried the old gentleman. And it was clear he meant to do it.

'Thank'ee,' said Scrooge. 'I am much obliged to you. I thank you fifty times. Bless you!'

He went to church, and walked about the streets, and watched the people hurrying to and fro, and patted children on the head, and questioned beggars, and looked down into the kitchens of houses, and up to the windows, and found that everything could yield him pleasure. He had never dreamed that any walk – that anything – could give him so much happiness. In the afternoon he turned his steps towards his nephew's house.

He passed the door a dozen times, before he had the courage to go up and knock. But he made a dash, and did it:

'Is you master at home, my dear?' said Scrooge to the girl. Nice girl! Very.

'Yes, sir.'

'Where is he, my love?' said Scrooge.

'He's in the dining-room, sir, along with mistress. I'll show you up-stairs, if you please.'

'Thank'ee. He knows me,' said Scrooge, with his hand already on the dining-room lock. 'I'll go in here, my dear.'

He turned it gently, and sidled his face in, round the door. They were looking at the table (which was spread out in great array); for these young housekeepers are always nervous on such points, and like to see that everything is right.

'Fred!' said Scrooge.

Dear heart alive, how his niece by marriage started! Scrooge had forgotten, for the moment, about her sitting in the corner with the footstool, or he wouldn't have done it, on any account.

'Why bless my soul!' cried Fred, 'who's that?'

'It's I. Your uncle Scrooge. I have come to dinner. Will you let me in, Fred?'

Let him in! It is a mercy he didn't shake his arm off. He was at home in five minutes. Nothing could be heartier. His niece looked just the same. So did Topper when *he* came. So did the plump sister, when *she* came. So did every one when *they* came. Wonderful party, wonderful games, wonderful unamimity, won-der-ful happiness!

But he was early at the office next morning. Oh, he was early there. If he could only be there first, and catch Bob Cratchit coming late! That was the thing he had set his heart upon.

And he did it; yes, he did! The clock struck nine. No Bob. A quarter past. No Bob. He was full eighteen minutes and a half behind his time. Scrooge sat with his door wide open, that he might see him come into the Tank.

His hat was off, before he opened the door; his comforter too. He was on his stool in a jiffy; driving away with his pen, as if he were trying to overtake nine o'clock.

'Hallo!' growled Scrooge, in his accustomed voice, as near as he could feign it. 'What do you mean by coming here at this time of day?'

'I am very sorry, sir,' said Bob. 'I *am* behind my time.'

'You are?' repeated Scrooge. 'Yes. I think you are. Step this way, sir, if you please.'

'It's only once a year sir,' pleaded Bob, appearing from the Tank. 'It shall not be repeated. I was making rather merry yesterday, sir.'

'Now, I'll tell you what, friend,' said Scrooge, 'I am not going to stand this sort of thing any longer. And therefore,' he continued, leaping from his stool, and giving Bob such a dig in the waistcoat that he staggered back into the Tank again: 'and therefore I am about to raise your salary!'

Bob trembled, and got a little nearer to the ruler. He had a momentary idea of knocking Scrooge down with it, holding him, and calling to the people in the court for help and a strait-waistcoat.

'A merry Christmas, Bob!' said Scrooge, with an earnestness that could not be mistaken, as he clapped him on the back. 'A merrier Christmas, Bob, my good fellow, than I have given you for many a year! I'll raise your salary, and endeavour to assist your struggling family, and we will discuss your affairs this very afternoon, over a

Christmas bowl of smoking bishop [mulled wine], Bob! Make up the fires, and buy another coal-scuttle before you dot another i, Bob Cratchit!'

Scrooge was better than his word. He did it all, and infinitely more; and to Tiny Tim, who did *not* die, he was a second father. He became as good a friend, as good a master, and as good a man, as the good old city knew, or any other good old city, town, or borough, in the good old world. Some people laughed to see the alteration in him, but he let them laugh, and little heeded them; for he was wise enough to know that nothing ever happened on this globe, for good, at which some people did not have their fill of laughter in the outset; and knowing that such as these would be blind anyway, he thought it quite as well that they should wrinkle up their eyes in grins, as have the malady in less attractive forms. His own heart laughed; and that was quite enough for him.

   He had no further intercourse with Spirits, but lived upon the Total Abstinence Principle, ever afterwards; and it was always said of him, that he knew how to keep Christmas well, if any man alive possessed the knowledge. May that be truly said of us, and all of us! And so, as Tiny Tim observed, God bless us, Every One!

 *hristmas Presents*

This is another custom which is said to have its origins in the Roman winter festival of Saturnalia. Romans used give their Emperor, and each other, tokens of good luck which they called *strenae*. This changed, in the way things do, and soon they were giving each other precious gifts of clothing and objects made of gold and silver.

The giving-at-Christmas tradition developed further with the story of the three wise kings and their gifts to the Christchild.

FROM

Christmas Childhood

PATRICK KAVANAGH

My father played the melodeon
Outside at our gate;
There were stars in the morning east
And they danced to his music.

Across the wild bogs his melodeon called
To Lennons and Callans.
As I pulled on my trousers in a hurry
I knew some strange thing had happened.

Outside in the cow-house my mother
Made the music of milking;
The light of her stable-lamp was a star
And the frost of Bethlehem made it twinkle.

A water-hen screeched in the bog,
Mass-going feet
Crunched the wafer-ice on the pot-holes,
Somebody wistfully twisted the bellows wheel.

My child poet picked out the letters
On the grey stone,
In silver the wonder of a Christmas townland,
The winking glitter of a frosty dawn.

Cassiopeia was over
Cassidy's hanging hill,
I looked and three whin bushes rode across
The horizon – the Three Wise Kings.

An old man passing said:
'Can't he make it talk' –
The melodeon. I hid in the doorway
And tightened the belt of my box-pleated coat.

I nicked six nicks on the door-post
With my penknife's big blade –
There was a little one for cutting tobacco.
And I was six Christmases of age.

My father played the melodeon,
My mother milked the cows,
And I had a prayer like a white rose pinned
On the Virgin Mary's blouse.

Merry Christmas

FROM
THE ISLANDMAN
TOMÁS Ó CROHAN

It was the morning of Christmas Eve. 'I fancy that I may as well go and get a sheep,' said I to my mother.

'Don't go,' says she. 'Give windy Diarmid his chance. We shall find out whether he comes up to his trumpeting. If he kills that big sheep there'll be enough for the two houses in her, but I'm afraid he won't make good his swaggering.'

She had far less confidence in him than I had. I expected that he'd keep his promise, if he did lay the big sheep low. He was a finished butcher, for those brothers had a big household when they kept house together. And often enough had the joker put a knife in a fine sheep of their flock without anybody telling him to.

I strolled out late in the evening to look if the cows were coming down from the hill, and what should I see but the rascal coming to the house with half the big sheep on his back. Diarmid had split the sheep so cleanly in two that half the head was still sticking to half the body.

When he went in, he threw off his load.

'There's a joint for you, little woman, for the Holy Day,' says he.

'May this day a year hence find you and us all in

prosperity and joy,' said she.
Just at that moment in I came. I looked at the present.
'Yerra, a blessing on your arms, good old uncle!' said I. 'You're a man of your word if anybody is.'
'Didn't I tell you that I'd do it?' said he. 'Sure, if it hadn't been for you and the help of God, I shouldn't have been alive to kill it. It's in honour of God that I killed it, and to share it with you. I shall never forget the seal's cave!'
I turned away from him and went to the box. I took out one of the four bottles that remained there, and came up to him.
'There, you've earned this drink to-day if you ever did, Diarmid.'
'Mary Mother! wherever did you get it all?' says he.
'Didn't you get a bottle from your friends yourself?'
'Devil a one except one my old friend Muirisin Bán gave me.'
Well, I filled him a glass and a half, for that was the full of the vessel I held in my hand.
'O, King of the Angels! don't you know that my old skeleton can't take in all that at one gulp after the day's toil?'
'This is the little Christmas drink.'
He seized the glass, and before long all its contents were in a place that kept them safe, and he said directly:
'I hope with God that we shall have a good Christmas and a good Shrove to follow.'
Then he jumped up and ran out through the door.
I ran after him and brought him in again.

'Yerra, aren't you in a hurry?' said I.

'O!' says he, 'to-night isn't like other nights, and it isn't right for me to fail my own little crowd on God's Blessed Eve.'

I'd always thought that he wasn't so devout as he showed himself that day, for he was always a rough-tongued chap, and it was his constant habit to go seeking help from hell whenever he was in a rage. His expression that day increased the respect I had for him. After a bit he went off.

When the time for lighting up came on 'God's Blessed Eve', if you were coming towards the village from the south-east – for that's the direction in which every door and window faces – and every kind of light is ablaze that night, you would imagine it a wing of some heavenly mansion, though it is set in the middle of the great sea. You would hear a noise in every house that night, for, however much or little drink comes to the Island, it is put aside for Christmas Eve. Maybe an old man would be singing who'd never lifted his voice for a year. As for the old women, they're always lilting away.

I felt that I would rather go out a bit than spend the whole evening at home. The place I meant to go to was Pat Heamish's house for a bit for he wasn't too well yet. I knew that he hadn't got a drop of drink, so I got a half-pint. There was a score or so of welcomes waiting for me. He was a man you could get a great deal of sport out of, but he was anything but happy, as he hadn't got a drop for Christmas. He'd drunk up all that he'd brought with him from Dingle, as his health had gone to pieces after the carouse.

I handed him the half-pint.

'Drink that down,' said I to him, 'for you've got to sing a song.'

'You'll get no song,' says Kate, 'if he once gets the half-pint down.'

'I'll sing a song, too,' says Tom.

He drank a tot and sang, not one song, but seven of them.

On Christmas Day and during the Christmas season we used to have hurley matches, and the whole village used to be mixed up in the game. Two men were chosen, one from each side, for captains. Each of them would call up man by man in turn until all who were on the strand were distributed in the two sides. We had hurleys and a ball. The game was played on the white Strand without shoes or stockings, and we went in up to our necks whenever the ball went into the sea. Throughout the twelve days of Christmas time there wasn't a man able to drive his cow to the hill for the stiffness in his back and his bones; a pair or so would have a bruised foot, and another would be limping on one leg for a month.

That Christmas Day my two uncles, Diarmid and Tom, were on opposite sides. I was on Diarmid's side, and that's where I preferred to be, for, if I had chanced to be against him, I couldn't have put out half my strength if I had been anywhere near him.

We won three games from them, one after another, and the two sides were raging – they struggling to win one game, anyhow, in the day and the other side swaggering. When we were approaching the cliff path on our way home, 'O, shame on you!' says uncle Diarmid, 'we didn't let you win a single game since morning.'

When Diarmid made that remark, his brother Tom was going up the path, just in front of him. He turned down, and raising his fist, gave him a blow in the ear-hole that sent him down on to the strand a cold corpse or nearly.

'Sure, you little devil, it wasn't you that did it.'

He hadn't far to fall, but it was rough ground. He lost his speech, if it was knocked clean out of him, and it was an hour before he could talk with all the others about him on the strand, all except the man who hit him – he'd gone home. Before long his feeble voice began to strengthen and when it came back he made no good use of it, for the first thing he said was: 'On my body and soul, I swear I'll be the priest at that fellow's deathbed!'

They set him on his feet, and he wasn't long in coming to himself. He only had a scratch or two on his cheek. We went off home, and it was as much as we could do, we were so tired after the day.

(Translated by Robin Flower)

Christmas Carol

G. K. CHESTERTON

The Christ-child lay on Mary's lap,
  His hair was like a light,
(O weary, weary were the world,
  But here is all aright.)

The Christ-child lay on Mary's heart,
  His hair was like a fire.
(O weary, weary is the world
  But here the world's desire.)

The Christ-child stood at Mary's knee,
  His hair was like a crown,
And all the flowers looked up at him,
  And all the stars looked down.

# Christmas Delicacies – US style

Make your own contribution to the season's over-abundance with an offering of Pecan Balls or a couple of pounds of Apricot Leather. Both are very popular Christmastime candies (sweets to you and me) in the US, the latter on the south-east seaboard especially.

For Pecan Balls simply sift together two tablespoons cocoa and one cup castor sugar. That done, stir in two tablespoons of apple juice and two tablespoons of corn syrup (maple or golden syrup will do). Now add two-and-a-half cups of crushed wafers and one cup broken pecan nuts. Make small balls of the mixture and sprinkle with castor sugar. Delicious.

Apricot Leather is made by putting a pound of dried apricots in three cups of boiling water and soaking for twelve hours. When they are well soaked, add two cups of sugar, bring to the boil and simmer for three quarters of an hour. Cool before emptying the mixture onto a board sprinkled with castor sugar. Begin rolling, a small section at a time, sprinkling with sugar if it sticks. Continue rolling and adding sugar until you have a thin sheet which looks like leather in texture. Cut into two-inch strips and roll these very tightly. The measures given should yield about two pounds of Apricot Leather. Store in an airtight biscuit tin.

The Friar's Christmas Night

SEAN HENRY

It was a cold dark Christmas night in 1847, the peak year of the terrible famine. An aged friar, the last of the Carmelite Friars from the now dying but once influential friary of Ballinsmall, two miles east of Claremorris, was hurrying on foot on the road from Claremorris to Knock. He was going in answer to a sick call to the village of Dalton about four miles north of Ballinsmall. He was accompanied by his neighbour and part-time servant Mark Gabhlain (or Forkan). Although their road was a Grand Jury road, as main trunk roads were then called, and was the road used by the Bianconi coaches plying between Sligo and Galway, it was rutted and dangerous after dark. On that account, they had to travel slowly in places and the friar's companion carried a military style lantern. This was something of a novelty as the only torches used by peasants in those days were live coals impaled on iron spikes or old reaping hooks.

A well known sheebeen stood at the junction of their road and another very old road at Barnacarroll. This other road was one of the roads that formed part of the Tochar Phadraig or pilgrim road that took pilgrims to Croaghpatrick. It was also an important road linking the old castles of Ballyhowley, Murneen and Brize. The forces of General Lake travelled over it in 1798 to retake Castlebar from the United Irishmen. On passing the sheebeen holding his lantern low to the ground, Mark Gabhlain observed two unusually bright-looking crowns close to the grass margin. Mark Gabhlain felt that the money was a Heaven-sent gift and that they should avail of it to get a tumbler or two of punch to help them on their way. In those days, the steaming bowl of whiskey punch was a popular remedy among the peasantry for most human ills. Nearly everybody had faith in a bowl of punch in its own good time, and in this regard, the friar was no exception.

The good friar hesitated, but only for a moment. He then bade his man to cover the crowns with two small flagstones from the road fence. 'If they are there,' 'he said, 'on our return, well and good.'

The friar arrived at his destination just in time and with not a minute to spare to anoint a young man who lay dying. He waited till all was over and the Rosary recited for the deceased before setting out on his return journey with his companion. He felt happy and kept thanking God that he had not yielded to temptation when passing the sheebeen, while Mark Gabhlain allowed himself visions of steaming punch when they got back to the sheebeen. When they got to the spot where they has seen the crowns, they found the flagstones undisturbed, to Mark's joy. He hastily lifted the stones. All he found was a large black *ciaróg* (cockroach) under each stone . . .

Sing Of A Maiden

ANON, FIFTEENTH CENTURY

I sing of a maiden
That is makeles;
King of all kings
To her son she ches.

He came al so still
There his mother was,
As dew in April
That falleth on the grass.

He came al so still
To his mother's bour,
As dew in April
That falleth on the flour.

He came al so still
There his mother lay,
As dew in April
That falleth on the spray.

Mother and maiden
Was never none but she;
Well may such a lady
Goddes mother be.

 *he Crib*

It's thought that St Francis of Assisi was responsible, in the thirteenth century, for the first nativity scene. It happened in Greccio, Italy, in 1223, and Mary, Joseph, the shepherds and the three kings were all represented by real people. The Christ Child, however, was made of wax.

St Francis's crib was a great hit and as time went on, nativity scenes became ever more elaborate. Figures were carved in wood or modelled from clay and were often dressed in rich fabrics and jewels. Some of these older cribs, now in museums, are priceless.

# The Christmas of Samuel Pepys

We had to dinner, my wife and I, a fine turkey and a mince-pie, and dined in state, poor wretch, she and I; and have thus kept our Christmas together, all alone almost – having not once been out. (*31 December 1633*)

To church, where our parson Mills made a good sermon. Then home, and dined well on some good ribbs of beef roasted and mince pies; only my wife, brother, and Barker, and plenty of good wine of my own; and my heart full of true joy and thanks to God Almighty for the goodness of my condition at this day. (*Christmas Day, 1666*)

# The Road To Heaven

GEORGE R. SIMS

How is the boy this morning? Why do you shake your head?
Ah! I can see what's happened – there's a screen drawn round the bed.
So poor little Mike is sleeping the last long sleep of all;
I'm sorry – but who would wonder, after that dreadful fall?

Let me look at him, doctor – poor little London waif!
His frail barque's out of the tempest, and lies in God's harbour safe;
It's better he died in the ward here, better a thousand times,
Than have wandered back to the alley, with its squalor and nameless crimes.

Too young for the slum to sully, he's gone to the wonderland
To look on the thousand marvels that he scarce could understand.
Poor little baby outcast, poor little waif of sin!
He has gone, and the pitying angels have carried the cripple in.

Didn't you know his story? – Ah, you weren't here, I
believe,
When they brought the poor little fellow to the hospital,
Christmas Eve.
It was I who came here with him, it was I who saw him go
Over the bridge that evening into the Thames below.

'Twas a raw cold air that evening – a biting Christmassy
frost –
I was looking about for a collie – a favourite dog I'd lost.
Some ragged boys, so they told me, had been seen with one
that night
In one of the bridge recesses, so I hunted left and right.

You know the stone recesses – with the long broad bench of
stone,
To many a weary outcast as welcome as monarch's throne;
On the fiercest night you may see them, as crouched in the
dark they lie.
Like the hunted vermin, striving to hide from the hounds in
cry.

The seats that night were empty, for the morrow was
Christmas Day,
And even the outcast loafers seemed to have slunk away;
They had found a warmer shelter – some casual ward,
maybe –
They'd manage a morning's labour for the sake of the meat
and tea.

I fancied the seats were empty, but, as I passed along,
Out of the darkness floated the words of a Christmas song,
Sung in a childish treble – 'twas a boy's voice hoarse with cold,
Quavering out the anthem of angels and harps of gold.

I stood where the shadows hid me, and peered about until
I could see two ragged urchins, blue with the icy chill,
Cuddling close together, crouched on a big stone seat –
Two little homeless arabs, waifs of the London street.

One was singing the carol, while the other, with big round eyes –
It was Mike – looked up in wonder, and said, 'Jack, when we dies
Is that the place as we goes to – that place where ye'r dressed in white?
And has golding 'arps to play on, and it's warm and jolly and bright?

'Is that what they mean by 'eaven, as the misshun coves talks about,
Where the children's always happy, and nobody kicks 'em out?'
Jack nodded his head, assenting, and then I listened and heard
The talk of the little arabs – listened to every word.

Jack was a Sunday scholar, so I gathered from what he said,
But he sang in the road for a living – his father and mother were dead;
And he had a drunken granny, who turned him into the street –
She drank what he earned, and often he hadn't a crust to eat.

He told little Mike of heaven in his rough, untutored way,
He made it a land of glory where the children sing all day;
And Mike, he shivered and listened, and told *his* tale to his friend,
How he was starved and beaten – 'twas a tale one's heart to rend.

He'd a drunken father and mother, who sent him out to beg,
Though he'd just got over a fever, and was lame with a withered leg;
He told how he daren't crawl homeward, because he had begged in vain,
And his parents' brutal fury haunted his baby brain.

'I wish I could go to 'eaven,' he cried, as he shook with fright;
'If I thought as they'd only take me, why I'd go this very night.
Which is the way to 'eaven? How d'ye get there, Jack?' –
Jack climbed on the bridge's coping, and looked at the water black.

'That there's *one* road to 'eaven,' he said, as he pointed down
To where the cold Thames water surged muddy and thick and brown.
'If we was to fall in there, Mike, we'd be dead; and right through there
Is the place where it's always sunshine, and the angels has crowns to wear.'

Mike rose and looked at the water; he peered in the big broad stream,
Perhaps with a childish notion he might catch the golden gleam
Of the far-off land of glory. He leaned right over and cried –
'If them are the gates of 'eaven, how I'd like to be inside!'

He'd stood but a moment looking – how it happened I cannot tell –
When he seemed to lose his balance, gave a short shrill cry, and fell –
Fell o'er the narrow coping, and I heard his poor head strike
With a thud on the stonework under; then splash in the Thames went Mike.

We brought him here that evening. For help I had
managed to shout —
A boat put off from the landing, and they dragged his
body out;
His forehead was cut and bleeding, but a vestige of life we
found;
When they brought him here he was senseless, but slowly
the child came round.

I came here on Christmas morning — the ward was all
bright and gay
With mistletoe, green, and holly, in honour of Christmas
Day;
And the patients had clean white garments, and a few in
the room out there
Had joined in a Christmas service — they were singing a
Christmas air.

They were singing a Christmas carol when Mike from his
stupor woke,
And dim on his wandering senses the strange surroundings
broke.
Half dreamily he remembered the tale he had heard from
Jack —
The song, and the while-robed angels, the warm bright
Heaven came back.

'I'm in Heaven,' he whispered faintly. 'Yes, Jack must
have told me true!'
And, as he looked about him, came the kind old surgeon
through.
Mike gazed at his face a moment, put his hand to his
fevered head,
Then to the kind old doctor, 'Please, are you God?' he
said.

Poor little Mike! 'twas Heaven, this hospital ward to him –
A heaven of warmth and comfort, till the flickering lamp
grew dim;
And he lay like a tired baby in a dreamless gentle rest,
And now he is safe for ever where such as he are best.

This is the day of scoffers, but who shall say that night,
When Mike asked the road to Heaven, that Jack didn't tell
him right?
'Twas the children's Jesus pointed the way to the kingdom
come
For the poor little tired arab, the waif of a London slum.

 # hristmas Cards

Surprisingly for something which has become an almost essential part of Christmas, the first cards didn't appear until the 1840s. It happened in England, where several families had cards printed and sent to their friends.

The real popularity of cards dates from 1875, after they were introduced in the US by a German emigrant printer.

he Fir Tree

TOVE JANSSON

One of the hemulens was standing on the roof, scratching at the snow. He had yellow woollen mittens that after a while became wet and disagreeable. He laid them on the chimney top, sighed and scratched away again. At last he found the hatch in the roof.

That's it, the hemulen said. And down there they're lying fast asleep. Sleeping and sleeping and sleeping. While other people work themselves silly just because Christmas is coming.

He was standing on the hatch, and as he couldn't remember whether it opened inwards or outwards he stamped on it, cautiously. It opened inwards at once, and the hemulen went tumbling down among snow and darkness and all the things the Moomin family had stowed away in the attic for later use.

The hemulen was now very annoyed and furthermore not quite sure of where he had left his yellow mittens. They were his favourite pair.

So he stumped down the stairs, threw the door open with a bang and shouted in a cross voice: 'Christmas's coming! I'm tired of you and your sleeping and now Christmas will be here almost any day!'

The Moomin family was hibernating in the drawing-room as they were wont to do. They had been sleeping for a few months already and were going to keep it up until spring. A sweet sleep had rocked them through what felt like a single long summer afternoon. Now all at once a cold draught disturbed Moomintroll's dreams. And someone was pulling at his quilt and shouting that he was tired and Christmas was coming.

'Is it spring already?' Moomintroll mumbled.

'Spring?' the hemulen said nervously. 'I'm talking about Christmas, don't you know, Christmas. And I've made absolutely no arrangements yet myself and here they send me off to dig you out. I believe I've lost my mittens. Everybody's running about like mad and nothing's ready . . . '

The hemulen clumped upstairs again and went out through the hatch.

'Mama, wake up!' Moomintroll said anxiously. 'Something's on. They call it Christmas.'

'What d'you mean?' his mother said and thrust her snout out from under the quilt.

'I don't really know,' her son replied. 'But nothing seems to be ready, and something's got lost, and all are running about like mad. Perhaps there's a flood again.'

He cautiously shook the Snork Maiden by the shoulder and whispered: 'Don't be afraid, but something terrible's happening.'

'Eh,' Moominpappa said. 'Easy now.'

He rose and wound the clock that had stopped somewhere in October.

Then they followed the hemulen's wet trail upstairs and climbed out on to the roof of the Moominhouse.

The sky was blue as usual, so this time it couldn't be the volcano. But all the valley was filled with wet cotton, the mountains and the trees and the river and the roof. And the weather was cold, much colder than in April.

'Is this the egg whites?' Moominpappa asked wonderingly. He scooped up some of the cotton in his paw and peered at it. 'I wonder if it's grown out of the ground,' he said. 'Or fallen down from the sky. If it came all at the same time that must have been most unpleasant.'

'But Pappa, it's snow,' Moomintroll said. 'I know it is, and it doesn't fall all at the same time.'

'No?' Moominpappa said. 'Unpleasant all the same.'

The hemulen's aunt passed by the house with a fir tree on her chair-sledge.

'So you're awake at last,' she observed casually. 'Better get yourself a fir before dark.'

'But why,' Moominpappa started to reply.

'I haven't time now,' the hemulen's aunt called back over her shoulder and quickly disappeared.

'Before dark, she said,' the Snork Maiden whispered. 'The danger comes by dark then.'

'And you need a fir tree for protection,' Moominpappa mused. 'I don't understand it.'

'Nor I,' Moominmamma said submissively. 'Put some woollen socks and scarfs on when you go for the fir. I'll make a good fire in the stove.'

Even if disaster was coming Moominpappa decided not to take one of his own firs, because he was particular about them. Instead he and Moomintroll climbed over Gaffsie's fence and chose a big fir she couldn't very well have any use for.

'Is the idea to hide oneself in it?' Moomintroll wondered.

'I don't know,' Moominpappa said and swung his axe. 'I don't understand a thing.'

They were almost by the river on their way back when Gaffsie came running towards them with a lot of parcels and paper bags in her arms.

She was red in the face and highly excited, so she did not recognise her fir tree, glory be.

'What a mill, what a fuss it all is!' Gaffsie cried.

'Badly brought-up hedgehogs should never be allowed to . . . And as I've told Misabel, it's a shame . . .'

'The fir,' Moominpappa said, desperately clinging to Gaffsie's fur collar. 'What does one do with one's fir?'

'Fir,' Gaffsie repeated confusedly. 'Fir? Oh, what a bother! Oh, how horrid . . . how on earth can I find the time . . .'

She dropped several parcels in the snow, her cap slipped askew and she was near to tears from pure nervousness.

Moominpappa shook his head and took hold of the fir again.

At home Moominmamma had dug out the verandah with a shovel and laid out life-belts, aspirin, Moominpappa's old gun and some warm compresses. One had to be prepared.

A small woody was sitting on the outermost edge of

the sofa, with a cup of tea in its paws. It had been sitting in the snow below the verandah, looking so miserable that Moominmamma had invited it in.

'Well, here's the fir,' Moominpappa said. 'If we only knew how to use it. Gaffsie said it had to be dressed.'

'We haven't anything large enough,' Moominmamma said worriedly. 'Whatever did she mean?'

'What a beautiful fir,' the small woody cried and swallowed some tea the wrong way down from pure shyness, regretting already that it had dared to speak.

'Do you know how to dress a fir tree?' the Snork Maiden asked.

The woody reddened violently and whispered: 'In beautiful things. As beautiful as you can. So I've heard.' Then, overwhelmed by its shyness, it clapped its paws to its face, upset the teacup and disappeared through the verandah door.

'Now keep quiet a moment, please, and let me think,' Moominpappa said. 'If the fir tree is to be dressed as beautifully as possible, then it can't be for the purpose of hiding in it. The idea must be to placate the danger in some way. I'm beginning to understand.'

They carried the fir out in the garden and planted it firmly in the snow. Then they started to decorate it all over with all the most beautiful things they could think up.

They adorned it with big shells from the summertime flowerbeds, and with the Snork Maiden's shell necklace. They took the prisms from the drawing-room chandelier and hung them from the branches, and at the very top they pinned a red silk rose that Moominpappa had once upon a time given Moominmamma as a present.

Everybody brought the most beautiful thing he had to placate the incomprehensible powers of winter.

When the fir tree was dressed the hemulen's aunt passed by again with her chair-sledge. She was steering the other way now, and her hurry was still greater.

'Look at our fir tree,' Moomintroll called to her.

'Dear me,' said the hemulen's aunt. 'But then you've always been a bit unlike other people. Now I must . . . I haven't the least bit of food ready for Christmas yet.'

'Food for Christmas,' Moomintroll repeated. 'Does he eat?'

The aunt never listened to him. 'You don't get away with less than a dinner at the very least,' she said nervously and went whizzing down the slope.

Moominmamma worked all afternoon. A little before dark she had the food cooked for Christmas, and served in small bowls around the fir tree. There was juice and yoghurt and blueberry pie and eggnog and other things the Moomin family liked.

'Do you think Christmas is very hungry?' Moominmamma wondered, a little anxiously.

'No worse than I, very likely,' Moominpappa said longingly. He was sitting in the snow with his quilt around his ears, feeling a cold coming on. But small creatures always have to be very, very polite to the great powers of nature.

Down in the valley all windows were lighting up. Candles were lit under the trees and in every nest among the branches, and flickering candle flames went hurrying through the snowdrifts. Moomintroll gave his father a questioning look.

'Yes,' Moominpappa said and nodded. 'Preparing for all eventualities.' And Moomintroll went into the house and collected all the candles he could find.

He planted them in the snow around the fir tree and cautiously lighted them, one after one, until all were burning in little circle to placate the darkness and Christmas. After a while everything seemed to quieten down in the valley; probably everyone had gone home to await what was coming. One single lonely shadow was wandering among the trees. It was the hemulen.

'Hello,' Moomintroll called softly. 'Is he coming?'

'Don't disturb me,' the hemulen replied sullenly, looking through a long list in which nearly every line seemed to be crossed out.

He sat down by one of the candles and started to count on his fingers. 'Mother, Father, Gaffsie,' he mumbled. 'The cousins ... the eldest hedgehog ... I can leave out the small ones. And Sniff gave me nothing last year. Then Misabel and Whomper, and auntie, of course ... This drives me mad.'

'What is it?' the Snork Maiden asked anxiously. 'Has anything happened to them?'

'Presents,' the hemulen exclaimed. 'More and more presents every time Christmas comes around!'

He scribbled a shaky cross on his list and ambled off.

'Wait!' Moomintroll shouted. 'Please explain ... And your mittens ... '

But the hemulen disappeared in the dark, like all the

others that had been in a hurry, and beside themselves over the coming of Christmas.

So the Moomin family quickly went in to look for some presents. Moominpappa chose his best trolling-spoon which had a very beautiful box. He wrote 'For Christmas' on the box and laid it out in the snow. The Snork Maiden took off her ankle ring and sighed a little as she rolled it up in silk paper.

Moominmamma opened her secret drawer and took out her book of paintings, the one and only coloured book in all the valley.

Moomintroll's present was so lavish and private that he showed it to no one. Not even afterwards, in the spring, did he tell anyone what he had given away.

Then they all sat down in the snow again and waited for the frightening guest.

Time passed, and nothing happened.

Only the small woody who had upset the cup of tea appeared from behind the woodshed. It had brought all its relations and the friends of these relations. Everyone was as small and grey and miserable and frozen.

'Merry Christmas,' the woody whispered shyly.

'You're the first to say some such thing,' Moominpappa said. 'Aren't you at all afraid of what's going to happen when Christmas comes?'

'This is it,' the woody mumbled and sat down in the snow with its relations. 'May we look? You've got such a wonderful fir tree.'

'And all the food,' one of the relations said dreamingly.

'And real presents,' said another.

'I've dreamed all my life of seeing this at close quarters,' the woody said with a sigh.

There was a pause. The candles burned steadily in the quiet night. The woody and its relations were sitting quite still. One could feel their admiration and longing, stronger and stronger, and finally Moominmamma edged a little closer to Moominpappa and whispered: 'Don't you think so too?'

'Why, yes, but if . . . ' Moominpappa objected.

'No matter,' Moomintroll said. 'If Christmas gets angry we can close the doors and perhaps we'll be safe inside.'

Then he turned to the woody and said: 'You can have it all.'

The woody didn't believe its ears at first. It stepped cautiously nearer to the fir tree, followed by all the relations and friends with devoutly quivering whiskers.

They had never had a Christmas of their own before.

'I think we'd better be off now,' Moominpappa said anxiously.

They padded back to the verandah, locked the door and hid under the table.

Nothing happened

After a while they looked anxiously out of the window.

All the small creatures were sitting around the fir tree, eating and drinking and opening parcels and have more fun than ever. Finally they climbed the fir and made fast the burning candles on the branches.

'Only there ought to be a star at the top,' the woody's uncle said.

'Do you think so?' the woody replied, looking thoughtfully at Moominmamma's red silk rose. 'What difference does it make once the idea's right?'

'The rose should have been a star,' Moominmamma whispered to the others. 'But how on earth?'

They looked at the sky, black and distant but unbelievably full of stars, a thousand times more than in summer. And the biggest one was hanging exactly above the top of their fir tree.

'I'm sleepy,' Moominmamma said. 'I'm really too tired to wonder about the meaning of all this. But it seems to have come off all right.'

'At least I'm not afraid of Christmas any more,' Moomintroll said. 'I believe the hemulen and his aunt and Gaffsie must have misunderstood the whole thing.'

They laid the hemulen's yellow mittens on the verandah rail where he'd be sure to catch sight of them, and then they went back to the drawing-room to sleep some more, waiting for the spring.

 # he Yuletide Log

We owe this tradition to the pagan, Germanic tribes who burnt a log during their winter solstice celebrations. Its name comes from *jol*, the Old Norse name for this festival. Later on, invaders from the north introduced the Yule log to England, helping to spread the tradition throughout Europe.

A proper Yule log, as distinct from the chocolate kind, should be big enough to burn for a long time. It is lit on Christmas Eve and people in some countries burn it little by little so that it will last until the New Year.

 n Austrian Christmas

MARIA VON TRAPP

Santa Claus does not come to the children of Austria. Nobody comes down the chimney to fill your stocking; it isn't so easy as that. All the small and big children of Austria have to write a letter addressed to the Christ Child on the first Sunday in Advent. He is believed to come down from heaven, Himself personally, on Christmas Eve, accompanied by angels and bring the Christmas tree and the wonderful things under it. This letter is a very important one, for in it you make known all your most secret wishes, and at the end you have to make a personal promise. Then you put it on the window-sill before going to bed, and next morning your first look will be to see whether your letter has gone. Good children's letters always disappear during the first night. Some children, however, have to wait two or three days, and if this should be the case with you, you really get quite anxious. It does help a lot in making you put your clothes tidily over a chair at night.

After the last carol, still sitting around the table, we started to write our Christmas letters. After a short thought I wrote down:

'Dear Christ Child: It would make my life so much

easier if You would bring each child here in the house a pair of nailed boots, a *Wetterfleck,* and a pair of wool mittens. I myself do not need anything, as I shall go back to Nonnberg soon anyway.'

The excitement of the first Sunday in Advent had hardly died down when the sixth of December came around, one of the most momentous days for all houses where children lived. On the vigil of this day Saint Nikolaus comes down to earth to visit all the little ones.

Saint Nikolaus was a saintly bishop of the fourth century, and as he was always very kind and helpful to children and young people, so God granted that every year on his feast-day he might come down to the children. He comes dressed in his Bishop's vestments, with a mitre on his head and his Bishop's staff in his hand. He is followed, however, by the Krampus, an ugly, black little devil with a long, red tongue, a pair of horns, and a long tail. When Saint Nikolaus enters a house, he finds the whole family assembled, waiting for him, and the parents greet him devoutly. Then he asks the children questions from their catechism. He makes them repeat a prayer or sing a song. He seems to know everything, all the dark spots of the past year, as you can see from his admonishing words. All the good children are given a sack with apples and nuts, prunes and figs, and the most delicious sweets. Bad children, however, must promise very hard to change their life. Otherwise, the Krampus will take them along, and he is grunting already and rattling his heavy chain. But the Holy Bishop won't ever let him touch a child. He believes the tearful eyes and stammered promises, but it may happen that, instead of a sweet bag, you get a switch. That will be put up in a conspicuous place and will look very symbolic of a child's behaviour.

The excitement was great on the fifth. Soon after dark we assembled in the hall, looking through the large window into the drive. Martina's hand was clasped tightly in mine, her little figure half hidden behind my skirt. You could almost hear Johanna's heart beating, and Hedwig's air of superiority was very unconvincing.

Suddenly one could see the little flicker of candlelight through the bare bushes. A tall figure bearing a lantern and high staff turned into our drive, followed at some distance by a little black fellow. The heavy double door opened wide, and in came the Holy Bishop, reverently greeted by young and old. The white beard which cascaded down below his waist showed his old age. Nobody could see that half an hour before, it had been plastered on Hans' patient face with the help of the white of a raw egg. Saint Nikolaus wore his glasses, as elderly people sometimes do, far down on his nose. He had to, because his eyesight was so good that Resi's spectacles almost blinded him. After he had sat down, he gave the Captain his lantern to hold, and then he produced from under his white cloak a large package with a big golden cross. Through the white paper cover one could read faintly Encyclopædia, *H. To HZ*. In this magic book were written down all the many crimes, big and little, which had been committed by the children of this house. It was quite incredible how well informed Saint Nikolaus was: how Werner had played truant three times instead of going to his Greek class; Hedwig had pinched

Martina; Rupert had smoked in secret; and Maria had practised the violin much longer than the doctor allowed; Resi, the cook, had burned the Sunday cake once and then thrown it into the garbage can without telling; Pepi, the gardener, was sometimes slow in getting up in the morning. And Saint Nikolaus shook his finger and frowned at the sinners as they were called to his feet. They all felt uncomfortable, and promised fervently to reform. The Holy Bishop rose and waved his hand towards the door; a big sack was pushed in, which Saint Nikolaus opened. There was a bag with fruit and candies for everybody except Resi, who got a large switch; and she even had to kiss the Bishop's hand when he gave it to her. With a final admonition and his blessing, the holy man left the house.

'How many days still until Christmas?' was the excited question every morning. One morning, when the answer was 'only seven,' we came down the stairs as usual, and found the double door leading into the big drawing-room, which was usually wide open, closed. New excitement; that meant that the Holy Child with His angel assistants was working inside, preparing the room for Christmas. From then on, the children only tiptoed in the vicinity of those closed doors, and every conversation downstairs died down to a reverent whisper.

The whispering continued deep into the night, when the children were long asleep and the Captain, Baroness Matilda, and I were busy behind the secret door with the still-empty Christmas tree, opening parcels, writing Christmas cards, adjusting small wax candles to small candle-holders which could be clamped on to the green branches. Slowly but surely, the big room began to look like the toy department of a large store. Out of the many-shaped parcels emerged all the blessings of our modern toy industry: a doll house and doll kitchen, a small perambulator with a beautiful baby and, of course, the whole outfit – diapers, bottle, bath-tub, etc.; picture books and games, an electric railroad, an air-gun, a gramophone with records, more books and more games, a new guitar, skates, skis – never in my life had I seen so many beautiful things in one spot. The trouble was that I could hardly keep my mind on my duty, which was to unpack and distribute, because it was so tempting to try out the new games, and look at the many books.

It was the twenty-third, and the little ones had sung all day long the traditional song, 'Morgen, Kinder, Wird's Was Geben'. They were unusually helpful, quiet and good, knowing that the house, and especially the nursery, was under constant observation by the angels coming and going to the Christmas room. Only Rupert and Agathe seemed to know a little more; from Maria down, the belief in the holy doings behind the wide doors was unshaken.

This last evening was devoted to the decoration of the tree. It was at least fifteen feet tall. The Captain, standing on a ladder, took care of the top, while Baroness Matilda and I busied ourselves with the lower branches. There were cakes, *Lebkuchen* and *Spanischer Wind*. Hard candles and chocolates had been wrapped in frilled tissue paper, figures and symbols made of marzipan, gilded nuts and small apples and tangerines, all these were hung on red threads all over the tree. Then came a hundred-and-twenty wax candles, loads of tinsel on the branches, and tinsel chains swinging loosely all around the tree. As a finishing touch the Captain fastened a large silver star to the very top. Then we all stepped back and admired the most beautiful Christmas tree I have ever seen in my life. The tables around the walls were so laden with presents that the white linen covers were completely hidden.

The next day was the big night, Holy Eve, as it is called in Austria. Snow had fallen overnight. We went to church with the older children. The church was filled as on Sunday. Everybody goes to confession on Holy Eve, so one had to wait in line. It was quite early and pitch-dark outside. There were no electric lights in the church, and, of course, it was not heated. The people had brought candles with them, fastened them to the pews, and, holding their hymn-books with heavily-mittened hands close to the little flame, they could read the words of the ancient Advent song, which was softly accompanied by the organ and sung by the whole community; 'Tauet Himmel den Gerechten.' In the flicker of candlelight one could see a neat little frosty cloud in front of every mouth. From under the choir loft, where the confessional stood, one could hear the shuffling of hobnailed boots and also, eventually, the rubbing of hands, the feeble attempts to keep warm when it was below zero outside with yard-long icicles growing from the church roof. But cold belonged to Christmas as heat to the haymaking days. This was as it should be and nobody gave it a thought.

hile Shepherds Watched Their Flocks By Night

NAHUM TATE

While shepherds watched their flocks by night,
    All seated on the ground,
The angel of the Lord came down,
    And glory shone around.

'Fear not,' said he, for mighty dread
    Had seized their troubled mind;
'Glad tidings of great joy I bring
    To you and all mankind.

'To you, in David's town, this day
    Is born of David's line,
The Saviour, who is Christ the Lord,
    And this shall be the sign:

'The Heavenly babe you there shall find
    To human view displayed
All meanly wrapped in swaddling bands,
    And in a manger laid.'

Thus spake the seraph; and forthwith
    Appeared a shining throng
Of angels, praising God, who thus
    Addressed their joyful song:

'All glory be to God on high,
    And to the earth be peace;
Good will henceforth from Heaven to men
    Begin and never cease.'

 # *hristmas Seals*

Like Christmas cards, these are a fairly recent innovation. The first seals were printed in Denmark in 1904, the brainwave of a postal clerk hoping to raise funds for a new children's hospital. They were sold in all Danish post offices and were such a success that other countries picked up on the idea. Seals continue to raise money for charities across the world.

 uireadh do Mhuire

MÁIRTÍN Ó DIREÁIN

An eol duit, a Mhuire,
Cá rachair i mbliana
  Ag iarraidh foscaidh
  Dod Leanbh Naofa,
  Tráth gach doras
  Dúnta Ina Éadan
  Ag fuath is uabhar
  An chine dhaonna?

Deonaigh glacadh
Le cuireadh uaimse
go hoileán mara
San iarthar chianda:
Beidh coinnle geala
I ngach fuinneoig lasta
Is tine mhóna
Ar theallach adhanta

Nollaig 1944

hristmas in Europe

In most European countries, the Christmas season begins on 6 December, the feast day of St Nicholas. In France he is called *Père Noël* and in the eastern parts of the country he visits children on his feastday. He arrives in other parts of France on Christmas Eve.

In Germany an early sign of Christmas is the Advent wreath which appears in churches on the first Sunday in Advent. A red candle is placed in the wreath each following Sunday so that on Christmas Day there will be four. The Christmas tree is not decorated until 24 December, when everyone gathers around it to exchange presents.

In Belgium and the Netherlands the fun begins on the evening of 6 December, when St Nicholas, on his white horse Sleipnir and dressed as a bishop, arrives with gifts. Children leave out hay, oats and carrots for Sleipnir and their shoes to have presents put into them.

A Comfortable Christmas

FROM
THE PICKWICK PAPERS
CHARLES DICKENS

From the centre of the ceiling of this kitchen, old Wardle had just suspended, with his own hands, a huge branch of mistletoe, and this same branch of mistletoe instantaneously gave rise to a scene of general and most delightful struggling and confusion; in the midst of which, Mr Pickwick, with a gallantry that would have done honour to a descendant of Lady Tollimglower herself, took the old lady by the hand, led her beneath the mystic branch, and saluted her in all courtesy and decorum. The old lady submitted to this piece of practical politeness with all the dignity which befitted so important and serious a solemnity, but the younger ladies, not being so thoroughly imbued with a superstitious veneration for the custom: or imagining that the value of a salute is very much enhanced if it cost a little trouble to obtain it: screamed and struggled, and ran into corners, and threatened and remonstrated, and did everything but leave the room, until some of the less adventurous gentlemen were on the point of desisting, when they all at once found it useless to resist any longer, and submitted to be kissed with a good grace.

Mr Wickle kissed the young lady with the black eyes, and Mr Snodgrass kissed Emily, and Mr Weller, not being particular about the form of being under the mistletoe, kissed Emma and the other female servants, just as he caught them. As to the poor relations, they kissed everybody, not even excepting the plainer portions of the young-lady visitors, who, in their excessive confusion, ran right under the mistletoe, as soon as it was hung up, without knowing it! Wardle stood with his back to the fire, surveying the whole scene, with the utmost satisfaction; and the fat boy took the opportunity of appropriating to his own use, and summarily devouring, a particularly fine mince-pie, that had been carefully put by, for somebody else.

Now, the screaming had subsided, and faces were in a glow, and curls in a tangle, and Mr Pickwick, after kissing the old lady as before mentioned, was standing under the mistletoe, looking with a very pleased countenance on all that was passing around him, when the young lady with the black eyes, after a little whispering with the other young ladies, made a sudden dart forward, and, putting her arm round Mr Pickwick's neck, saluted him affectionately on the left cheek; and before Mr Pickwick distinctly knew what was the matter, he was surrounded by the whole body, and kissed by every one of them.

It was a pleasant thing to see Mr Pickwick in the centre of the group, now pulled this way, and then that, and first kissed on the chin, and then on the nose, and then on the spectacles: and to hear the peals of laughter which were raised on every side; but it was a still more pleasant thing to see Mr Pickwick, blinded shortly afterwards with a silk handkerchief, falling up against the wall, and scrambling into corners, and going through all the mysteries of blind-man's buff, with the utmost relish for the game, until at last he caught one of the poor relations, and then had to evade the blind-man himself, which he did with a nimbleness and agility that elicited the admiration and applause of all beholders. The poor relations caught the people who they thought would like it, and, when the game flagged, got caught themselves. When they were all tired of blind-man's buff, there was a great game at snap-dragon, and when fingers enough were burned with that, and all the raisins were gone, they sat down by the huge fire of blazing logs to a substantial supper, and a mighty bowl of wassail, something smaller than an ordinary wash-house copper, in which the hot apples were hissing and bubbling with a rich look, and a jolly sound, that were perfectly irresistible.

'This,' said Mr Pickwick, looking round him, 'this is, indeed, comfort.'

 *anta on the Internet*

GORDON SNELL

Old Santa Claus was busy
Putting presents on his sleigh:
'There's the football boots for Damien
And the bicycle for Kay.
Jane asked me for a terrier
And Jason for a toad.
With all these gifts I fear the sleigh
Will hardly bear the load.'

He sighed, 'It's quite exhausting,
Though it *is* a worthy cause.'
The Snow Queen laughed and told him:
'Get with it Santa Claus!
Have your letters sent by E-Mail –
And those modern kids, I bet,
Would rather Father Christmas
Arrived by Internet!'

Soon Santa's Cave was crowded
With computers and their screens,
And no-one could hear 'Jingle Bells'
For the bleeping of machines.
Santa tapped the keyboards,
And the screens were all a-glow.
He beamed himself around the Net
With a booming 'Ho! Ho! Ho!'

The reindeer stood and watched him
And one said with a sob:
'Now Santa's on the Internet
We haven't got a job!'
Just then a robin landed –
A disc was in his beak.
He said: 'A child sent this, to say
She's finding Christmas bleak.'

The message came from Jenny:
'Dear Santa, I can't pat
The present that you sent me –
A computer graphic's cat!
I try to kiss and hug her
And stroke her glossy hair,
Then sadly I discover
She isn't really there.'

'They say the Net's a wonder,'
Said Santa, 'and they're right,
But you cannot play with modems
Or stroke a megabyte.
You can do a lot with Windows,
But Chimneys are *my* way –
So saddle up the reindeer
And load the Christmas sleigh.

'Yes, the Internet's a wonder
But it really would be shocking
If the age of electronics
Meant an empty Christmas stocking.'
The reindeer were delighted –
There was cheering and applause
As the children welcomed
The return of Santa Claus!

 hristmas Carols

The first carol, according to tradition, was sung by the angels who announced the birth of Christ to the shepherds outside Bethlehem. The history books, on the other hand, say that carols come from the middle ages and that the word itself comes from the Old French *carole*, a round dance accompanied by singing. The earliest printed Christmas carol was 'The Boar's Head' (1512), which is still sung each year at Oxford. More than 500 English carols survive from the fifteenth century.

 ngel Children

FROM
LITTLE WOMEN
BY LOUISA MAY ALCOTT

Jo was the first to wake in the grey dawn of Christmas morning. No stockings hung at the fireplace, and for a moment she felt as much disappointed as she did long ago, when her little sock fell down because it was so crammed with goodies. Then she remembered her mother's promise, and, slipping her hand under her pillow, drew out a little crimson-covered book. She knew it very well, for it was that beautiful old story of the best life ever lived, and Jo felt that it was a true guide-book for any pilgrim going the long journey. She woke Meg with a 'Merry Christmas', and bade her see what was under her pillow. A green-covered book appeared, with the same picture inside, and a few words written by their mother, which made their one present very precious in their eyes. Presently Beth and Amy woke, to rummage and find their little books also – one, dove-coloured, the other blue; and all sat looking at and talking about them, while the east grew rosy with the coming day.

In spite of her small vanities, Margaret had a sweet and pious nature, which unconsciously influenced her sisters, especially Jo, who loved her very tenderly, and obeyed her because her advice was so gently given.

'Girls,' said Meg seriously, looking from the tumbled head beside her to the two little night-capped ones in the room beyond, 'Mother wants us to read and love and mind these books, and we must begin at once. We used to be faithful about it; but since Father went away, and all this war trouble unsettled us, we have neglected many things. You can do as you please; but *I* shall keep my book on the table here, and read a little every morning as soon as I wake, for I know it will do me good, and help me through the day.'

Then she opened her new book and began to read. Jo put her arm round her, and, leaning cheek to cheek, read also, with the quiet expression so seldom seen on her restless face.

'How good Meg is! Come, Amy, let's do as they do. I'll help you with the hard words, and they'll explain things if we don't understand,' whispered Beth, very much impressed by the pretty books and her sister's example.

'I'm glad mine is blue,' said Amy; and then the rooms were very still while the pages were softly turned, and the winter sunshine crept in to touch the bright heads and serious faces with a Christmas greeting.

'Where is Mother?' asked Meg, as she and Jo ran down to thank her for their gifts, half an hour later.

'Goodness only knows. Some poor creeter come a-beggin', and your ma went straight off to see what was needed. There never *was* such a woman for givin' away vittles and drink, clothes, and firin',' replied Hannah, who had lived with the family since Meg was born, and was considered by them all more as a friend than a servant.

'She will be back soon, I think; so fry your cake, and have everything ready,' said Meg, looking over the presents which were collected in a basket and kept under the sofa, ready to be produced at the proper time. 'Why, where is Amy's bottle of cologne?' she added, as the little flash did not appear.

'She took it out a minute ago, and went off with it to put a ribbon on it, or some such notion,' replied Jo, dancing about the room to take the first stiffness off the new army-slippers.

'How nice my handkerchiefs look, don't they! Hannah washed and ironed them for me, and I marked them all myself,' said Beth, looking proudly at the somewhat uneven letters which had cost her such labour.

'Bless the child! She's gone and put 'Mother' on them instead of 'M. March'. How funny!' cried Jo, taking up one.

'Isn't it right? I thought it was better to do it so, because Meg's initials are "M. M." ', and I don't want anyone to use these but Marmee,' said Beth, looking troubled.

'It's all right, dear, and a very pretty idea – quite sensible, too, for one can never mistake now. It will please her very much, I know,' said Meg, with a frown for Jo and a smile for Beth.

'There's Mother. Hide the basket, quick!' cried Jo, as a door slammed, and steps sounded in the hall.

Amy came in hastily, and looked rather abashed when she saw her sisters all waiting for her.

'Where have you been, and what are you hiding behind you?' asked Meg, surprised to see, by her hood and cloak, that Lazy Amy had been out so early.

'Don't laugh at me, Jo! I didn't mean anyone should know till the time came. I only meant to change the little bottle for a big one, and I gave *all* my money to get it, and I'm truly trying not to be selfish any more.'

As she spoke, Amy showed the handsome flask which replaced the cheap one; and looked so earnest and humble in her little effort to forget herself that Meg hugged her on the spot, and Jo pronounced her 'a trump', while Beth ran to the window and picked her finest rose to ornament the stately bottle.

'You see, I felt ashamed of my present, after reading and talking about being good this morning, so I ran round the corner and changed it the minute I was up; and I'm *so* glad, for mine is the handsomest now.'

Another bang of the street door sent the basket under the sofa, and the girls to the table, eager for breakfast.

'Merry Christmas, Marmee! Many of them! Thank you for our books; we read some, and mean to, every day,' they cried, in chorus.

'Merry Christmas, little daughters! I'm glad you began at once, and hope you will keep on. But I want to say one word before we sit down. Not far away from here lies a poor woman with a little new-born baby. Six children are huddled into one bed to keep from freezing, for they have no fire. There is nothing to eat over there; and the oldest boy came to tell me they were suffering hunger and cold. My girls, will you give them your breakfast as a Christmas present?'

They were all unusually hungry, having waited nearly

an hour, and for a minute no one spoke; only for a minute, for Jo exclaimed impetuously:

'I'm so glad you came before we began!'

'May I go and help carry the things to the poor little children?' said Beth, eagerly.

'*I* shall take the cream and the muffins,' added Amy, heroically, giving up the articles she most liked.

Meg was already covering the buckwheats, and piling the bread into one big plate.

'I thought you'd do it,' said Mrs March, smiling as if satisfied. 'You shall all go and help me, and when we come back we will have bread and milk for breakfast, and make it up at dinner-time.'

They were soon ready, and the procession set out. Fortunately it was early, and they went through back streets, so few people saw them, and no one laughed at the queer party.

A poor, bare, miserable room it was, with broken windows, no fire, raged bed-clothes, a sick mother, wailing baby, and a group of pale, hungry children cuddled under one old quilt, trying to keep warm.

How the big eyes stared and blue lips smiled as the girls went in!

'*Ach, meim Goff!* It is good angels come to us!' said the poor woman, crying for joy.

'Funny angels in hoods and mittens,' said Jo, and set them laughing.

In a few minutes it really did seem as if kind spirits had been at work there. Hannah, who had carried wood, made a fire, and stopped up the broken panes with old hats and her own cloak. Mrs March gave the mother tea and gruel, and comforted her with promises of help, while she dressed the little baby as tenderly as if it had been her own. The girls, meantime, spread the table, set the children round the fire, and fed them like so many hungry birds – laughing, talking, and trying to understand the funny broken English.

'*Das ist gut!*' '*Die Engelkinder!*' cried the poor things, as they ate, and warmed their purple hands at the comfortable blaze.

The girls had never been called angel children before, and thought it very agreeable, especially Jo, who had been considered a 'Sancho' ever since she was born. That was a very happy breakfast, though they didn't get any of it; and when they went away, leaving comfort behind, I think there were not in all the city four merrier people than the hungry little girls who gave away their breakfasts and contented themselves with bread and milk on Christmas morning.

'That's loving our neighbour better than ourselves, and I like it,' said Meg, as they set out their presents, while their mother was upstairs collecting clothes for the poor Hummels.

Not a very splendid show, but there was a great deal of love done up in the few little bundles; and the tall vase of red roses, white chrysanthemums, and trailing vines, which stood in the middle, gave an elegant air to the table.

'She's coming! Strike up, Beth! Open the door, Amy! Three cheers for Marmee!' cried Jo, prancing about, while Meg went to conduct Mother to the seat of honour.

Beth played her gayest march, Amy threw open the door, and Meg enacted escort with great dignity. Mrs March was both surprised and touched; and smiled with her eyes full as she examined her presents, and read the little notes which accompanied them. The slippers went on at once, a new handkerchief was slipped into her pocket, well scented with Amy's cologne, the rose was fastened in her bosom, and the nice gloves were pronounced a 'perfect fit'.

There was a good deal of laughing and kissing and explaining, in the simple, loving fashion which makes these home festivals so pleasant at the time, so sweet to remember long afterwards, and then all fell to work.

The morning charities and ceremonies took so much time that the rest of the day was devoted to preparations for the evening festivities.

The Christmas-Tree

JULIA GODDARD

   It grew in the woods,
      And the sun shone down,
   And crowned its head
      With a golden crown.
Every morning and every night
The fir-tree stood in a blaze of light:
Hurrah for the fir-tree, the Christmas-tree!
A prince in all the forests is he.

   It grew for Christmas,
      It raised its head,
   'The fir-tree to glory
      Will come,' the wind said.
The woodman came and bore it away,
And the wind soft whispered of Christmas Day:
Hurrah for the fir-tree, the Christmas-tree!
A prince in all the forests is he.

The fir-tree stood
In a beautiful room:
A hundred tapers
Dispelled the gloom.
All decked with gold and silver was he,
And lilies, and roses so fair to see:
Hurrah for the fir-tree, the Christmas-tree!
A prince in all the forests is he.

Wide spread his branches,
And bending low
With toys and trinkets,
A goodly show:
'The wealth of the Indies is mine,' said he;
And the children peeped in at the Christmas-tree:
Hurrah for the fir-tree, the Christmas-tree!
A prince in all the forests is he.

The little children,
With merry shout,
Came crowding, clustering
Round about;
Brighter and rounder grew their eyes,
And they gazed at the fir-tree in glad surprise:
Hurrah for the fir-tree, the Christmas-tree!
A prince in all the forests is he.

The fir-tree listened
  With branches bent,
And drank in their praises
  With sweet content.
With pride and pleasure his heart beat fast,
For he knew that his glory had come at last:
Hurrah for the fir-tree, the Christmas-tree!
A prince in all the forests is he.

lory to God in the Highest

LUKE 2: 1-20

And it came to pass in those days, that there went out a decree from Caesar Augustus, that all the world should be taxed. (And this taxing was first made when Cyrenius was governor of Syria.) And all went to be taxed, every one into his own city. And Joseph also went up from Galilee, out of the city of Nazareth, into Judaea, unto the city of David, which is called Bethlehem; (because he was of the house and lineage of David:) to be taxed with Mary his espoused wife, being great with child. And so it was that while they were there, the days were accomplished that she should be delivered. And she brought forth her firstborn son, and wrapped him in swaddling clothes, and laid him in a manger; because there was no room for them in the inn. And there were in the same country shepherds abiding in the field, keeping watch over their flock by night. And, lo, the angel of the Lord came upon them, and the glory of the Lord shone round about them: and they were sore afraid. And the angel said unto them, Fear not: for behold, I bring you tidings of great joy, which shall be to all people. For unto you is born this day in the city of David a Saviour, which is Christ the Lord. And this shall be a sign unto you; Ye shall find the babe wrapped in swaddling clothes, lying in a manger. And suddenly there was with the angel a multitude of heavenly host praising God, and saying, Glory to God in the highest, and on earth, good will toward men.

 *deste, fideles*

Adeste, fideles,
Laeti triumphantes;
Venite, venite in Bethlehem . . .
O come, all ye faithful,
Joyful and triumphant,
O come ye, O come ye to Bethlehem . . .

Biographical Index

LOUISA MAY ALCOTT was born in Germanstown, Philadelphia in 1832 and worked as a nurse in a Union hospital during the Civil War. In 1868 she achieved an enormous success with her children's classic *Little Women,* which was based upon her own family life, herself the model for the tomboy Jo. She followed it with other popular books about the March family including *Good Wives* (1869), *Little Men* (1871) and *Jo's Boys* (1886). She died in 1888.

HANS CHRISTIAN ANDERSEN was born in 1805 in Odense in the Danish island of Fyn, the son of a poor shoemaker. After his father's death he moved to Copenhagen, trying unsuccessfully for work in the theatre and as a singer. Eventually he was able to complete his education with the grant of royal scholarships and made a reasonable living as a writer. His tales for children, notably 'The Tin Soldier', 'The Emperor's New Clothes', 'The Snow Queen' and 'The Ugly Duckling' have made him world famous. He died in 1875.

MAEVE BINCHY was born in Dalkey, County Dublin in 1940 and educated at UCD. She taught for eight years (1960–8) and then became a journalist with *The Irish Times,* for which she still writes a regular column. She has published several collections of short stories and has achieved enormous success with a number of novels beginning with *Light a Penny Candle* (1982).

G[ILBERT] K[EITH] CHESTERTON was born in London in 1874 and educated at St Paul's School and later at the Slade School of Art. He became a journalist and soon earned a worldwide reputation as an essayist, poet, novelist and critic. He became a Catholic in 1922 and the priest who instructed him became the model for his most famous creation 'Father Brown', the theologian detective. He died in 1936.

CHARLES DICKENS was born near Portsmouth in 1812 but moved to Chatham when he was four. His family fell into debt and he, a highly intelligent and deeply sensitive child, was forced to work in a blacking factory in London when he was twelve. He became a parliamentary reporter with the reputation as the swiftest and the most accurate shorthand taker of House of Commons debates. His literary career began with a series of sketches written under the pseudonym of 'Boz'. By the age of twenty five he was one of the most popular authors in the English-speaking world. He wrote incessantly, producing in all fourteen novels (including the unfinished *The Mystery of Edwin Drood*) many essays, sketches and stories. He had high blood pressure and it is likely that his highly lucrative and utterly gripping dramatic readings from his own works hastened his death, which occurred at his home in Gadshill, Kent in 1870. He was the premier nineteenth-century novelist but not really a Victorian. He is considered the only rival of Shakespeare in his creation of character, humour, use of language and human sympathy.

JULIA GODDARD, who died in 1896, wrote 'The Christmas Tree' for the children's magazine *Little Folks* of December 1880.

GEORGE GROSSMITH was born in 1847. He was a journalist, writer, entertainer and singer, connected especially with Gilbert and Sullivan operettas. His brother WEEDON GROSSMITH was born in 1854, trained as a painter but spent most of his life working in the theatre, as playwright, manager and also as actor specialising in 'Pooteresque' characters. Weedon Grossmith illustrated *The Diary of a Nobody*, which he co-wrote with his brother.

SEAN HENRY was born in Ballydrum, County Mayo in 1906 and emigrated to America in 1924, returning home in 1931. He worked with Mayo County Council, retiring as a waterworks supervisor.

ISAIAH (8th century BC) son of Amos, was one of the prophets of the Old Testament. He was martyred sometime after the Assyrian invasion of 701 BC.

TOVE JANSSON was born in Finland in 1914 and is famous as the inventor of the Finn Family Moomintroll which tells and pictures the fantastic world of the Moomins. Her books and comic strips have gained worldwide popularity and have won her many prizes. She has also written for adults.

JAMES JOYCE was born in Dublin in 1882 and educated at Clongowes, Belvedere and UCD. He left Ireland for more or less permanent exile in 1904, living in Trieste, Zürich and Paris. His collection of short stories *Dubliners* (1914) made him famous and by the time the autobiographical *A Portrait of the Artist as a Young Man* appeared in 1915 he was recognised as a modern master, a judgement confirmed by *Ulysses* (1922), one of the greatest novels of all time. He died in Zürich in 1941.

ÉAMON KELLY was born near Killarney in County Kerry in 1941 and after some time spent teaching woodwork, became a member of the Drama department of Radio Éireann, eventually joining the Abbey Theatre. He is famous for his stories both written and oral and is probably Ireland's leading *seanchaí*. He is the author of six collections of stories and an autobiography, *The Apprentice*.

ST LUKE was a Greek, and therefore a gentile, born in Antioch, Syria sometime during the first century AD. Tradition has it that he was a physician, referred to as such by St Paul whom he accompanied on some of his missionary journeys. He died at age eighty-four in Greece, having written the most literary of the gospels and the only one in Greek. He was also a painter, though the images of the Blessed Virgin ascribed to him belong to a much later period. He is the patron of doctors and artists and his symbol is the winged ox.

MÁIRE MHAC AN TSAOI was born in Dublin in 1922 and after qualifying as a barrister joined the Department of External Affairs. She is one of Ireland's leading Gaelic poets and has won many prizes. She is married to Conor Cruise O'Brien.

CLEMENT CLARKE MOORE was born in New York in 1779. He was principal lecturer in Hebrew in the General Theological Seminary there and wrote his famous poem 'A Visit from St Nicholas' for his family's pleasure in 1822. It was first published in the *Troy Sentinel* on 23 December 1823. Moore died in Newport, Rhode Island in 1863.

JOHN JULIUS NORWICH was born in 1929, the son of Viscount Norwich and Lady Diana Cooper. He succeeded to the title in 1954, by which time he was in the Foreign Service. He resigned in 1964 in order to write mainly history books, notably of the Venetian republic. Married to a painter, he has two children and takes the Liberal whip in the House of Lords.

TOMÁS Ó CROHAN (aka Ó Criomhthain) was born and lived all his life on the Great Blasket off the Dunquin peninsula in County Kerry in 1856. At the urging of mainland scholars, notably Robin Flower and Brian Ó Cheallaigh, he wrote an account of daily island life called *Allagar na hInise* which was published in 1928. This was followed in 1929 by *An tOileánach*, his autobiography, which was immediately recognised as a major work in the Irish language. He died in 1937.

MÁIRTÍN Ó DIREÁIN was born in Inis Mór, the largest of the Aran Islands, in 1910 and joined the postal service in 1928. He acted in the Taibhdhearc in Galway before being transferred to Dublin, where he worked in the postal censorship department during the war. He is considered one of the most powerful of the modern Irish poets, finding his main inspiration in memories of his island home. He died in 1988.

SAMUEL PEPYS was born in 1633, the son of a London tailor. Educated at St Paul's School and Magdalene College, Cambridge, he became secretary to the Admiralty in 1672, having risen rapidly as one of Charles II's bright young men of the Restoration. His famous diary, kept in cipher from 1660 to 1669 is a marvellously frank account of his private and public life and gives graphic descriptions of the the three great disasters of the decade – the great plague (1665-6), the great fire of London (1666) and the triumphal procession of the enemy Dutch fleet (under De Ruyter) up the Thames. Pepys died in 1703.

CHRISTINA ROSSETTI was born in London in 1830, the younger sister of Dante Gabriel Rossetti, one of the founders of the art movement known as the Pre-Raphaelite Brotherhood. A High Anglican, she broke off her engagement because her fiancé became a Roman Catholic. Though often ill she lived until 1894. Her lyric poems are very powerful and one, 'In the Bleak Midwinter', has become a standard Christmas carol.

GEORGE R[OBERT] SIMS was born in London in 1847 and educated in Germany. He began his literary career as a humorous journalist but became famous as the author, under the pseudonym 'Dagonet', of a number of famous dramatic recitations, notably the often-parodied 'In the Workhouse: Christmas Day'. During his career he wrote many novels of London life and a number of plays. He was a social reformer with aristocratic tastes and invented a hair-restorer called Tatcho, named after his publisher Chatto. He died in 1922.

ROBERT LOUIS STEVENSON was born in Edinburgh in 1850, the son of a lighthouse engineer. Of poor health, he gave up his engineering studies to study law, becoming an advocate in 1875. He wrote many stories and sketches but he did not achieve any recognition until the publication of the romantic adventure story *Treasure Island* in 1883. This was followed by his finest book, *Kidnapped,* in 1886 and the same year saw his famous horror story *The Strange Tale of Dr Jekyll and Mr Hyde*. In 1889 he left for the Samoa hoping to cure his tuberculosis. He died there in 1894.

NAHUM TATE was born in Dublin in 1652 and educated at TCD. He moved to London and became both playwright and play doctor, giving *King Lear* a happy ending whereby Cordelia marries Edgar. He succeeded Thomas Shadwell as Poet Laureate in 1692 and died in poverty in 1715.

MARIA VON TRAPP was governess and later stepmother of the children of the Austrian naval captain, Baron Von Trapp. After the Anschluss in 1938 they escaped from the Nazis by climbing the Alps into Switzerland and later emigrated to America. The story of Maria and the family of singers was the basis of the Rodgers and Hammerstein Broadway musical *The Sound of Music*, which became an immensely popular film in 1965.

Acknowledgements

For permission to reproduce copyright material the editor and publishers are grateful to the following: Viscount John Julius Norwich for 'The Twelve Days of Christmas, a Correspondence'; A&C Black Ltd for 'The Fir Tree' by Tove Jansson; John Johnson Agents Ltd for 'Santa on the Internet' copyright © Gordon Snell 1995; Christine Green Authors' Agent for 'The Fat Boy's Christmas' copyright © Maeve Binchy 1995; Oxford University Press for 'A Merry Christmas' from *The Islandman* by Thomas Ó Crohan translated by Robin Flower copyright © Robin Flower 1991; the trustees of the Estate of Patrick Kavanagh, c/o Peter Fallon, Literary Agent, Loughcrew, Oldcastle, County Meath, Ireland for an extract from 'A Christmas Childhood' by Patrick Kavanagh; the estate of Patricia Lynch for 'Last Bus for Christmas' from *The Genius*, copyright © Patricia Lynch; Sairséal Ó Marcaigh for 'Cuireadh do Mhuire' by Máirtín Ó Díreáin and 'Oíche Nollag' by Máire Mhac an tSaoi; Mercier Press for 'The Season of Light' by Éamon Kelly and 'The Friar's Christmas' by Sean Henry.

Every effort has been made to trace copyright holders. The Publishers regret any errors or omissions in the above acknowledgements.